PRAISE FOR *HC*

"Kevin Moore has delivered a tremendous resource, teaching us how to reveal God's love to our church family. Just as Charles Ryrie's *Balancing the Christian Life* is essential reading for the growing disciple, so is Kevin Moore's *Holy Rebellion* similarly impactful for the pastor. These biblical truths run deeper than a wholesome formula to love your church; this book is a treatise on how to balance the pastor's life."

Bruce McCoy, D.Min.
Southwestern Seminary
President of the Missouri Baptist Convention (2008–2010)

"As Kevin's assistant, I have listened to him explain and watched him model the faithful path he endorses in this book. If you are a new pastor like me, you may tend to think of issues before people, to rush ahead of those you lead, or wrongly to pit biblical fidelity against deliberate patience as you earn your people's trust. If so, you will benefit from this book. May the Lord use *Holy Rebellion* to inspire you to glorify Him by practicing the loving pastoring I have witnessed from Kevin in person."

Dallas Vandiver
Pastoral Assistant, Lamar Baptist Church, Arlington, TX

"Dr. Moore's book is written from great insight and experience. It is a must read for every new pastor and one that will be greatly appreciated by those already in ministry positions. You will enjoy the mixture of humor and candor interwoven within the context of the book."

Mike Evans, Th.D.
Former President of the World Baptist Fellowship
Chairman of WBV Mission Agency Board
Co-Founder of Iron Men Ministries

"After fifty-six years of ministry, I have read many books and Kevin Moore's book, *Holy Rebellion*, is one of the best dealing with pastoral ministry. His honesty is so refreshing. He goes to the very heart of what Jesus has taught us to be and do."

Johnny Irish
Retired Elder of the United Methodist Church

"From the very first page the words connected with my heart. What a testimony of how to love your church. But this book is more than that. It is straightforward, it is insightful, and it is encouraging. Thoughts I've had about ministry for years but was never able to put into words suddenly seemed to crystalize in my mind, but there was more. Kevin expanded the horizon of my thoughts and probed the depths of my heart, prompting me to ask the difficult question, am I truly loving my church as I should?"

Jim Tucker
Pastor, First Baptist Church Everman

"Within these pages . . . you will find the voice of a pastor humorously and humbly exemplifying what it means to 'shepherd the flock of God among you' so that 'when the Chief Shepherd appears, you will receive the unfading crown of glory'" (1 Peter 5:2, 4).

John B. Mann
Pastor LaJunta Baptist Church
Springtown, TX

"Dr. Moore provides superb wisdom for pastors in the first book of its kind I have seen. I wish I had had Dr. Moore's wisdom in the early days of my ministry. Pastors, move this book to the top of your reading list."

Waylan Owens, Ph.D.
Dean of the Church and Family Ministries, Southwestern Seminary
Fort Worth, TX

"*Holy Rebellion* is one of the best books I have ever read. The message will encourage and inspire all ministers, from rookies to seasoned veterans. This honest and refreshing read provides relatable examples and practical, scripturally based advice for loving and leading God's people in all circumstances. *Holy Rebellion* should be required reading at all seminaries. Churches should require interns to read this book. I was inspired."

Jon Lineberger, Ed.D.
Assistant Vice President, Dallas Baptist University
Author of *What God Did with a Mess Like Me*

"Dr. Kevin Moore knows the pastorate. He knows the great joys, the great struggles, the great successes, and even the mistakes one can make. This book should be the gift for every young pastor about to begin his first jaunt in the pastoral field. From the city to the countryside, from old established churches to new church plants, people want you to love them. And if you love them, they will follow you. Allow *Holy Rebellion* to inform your thinking on how to love your church, in every situation."

Ryan Jespersen
Director, Urban Missions
Baptist General Convention of Texas
Dallas, TX

HOLY REBELLION:

REDEFINING EXCELLENCE IN PASTORAL MINISTRY

KEVIN J. MOORE, Ph.D.

FOREWORD BY

PAIGE PATTERSON

Collierville, Tennessee

Published by
Innovo Publishing, LLC
www.innovopublishing.com
1-888-546-2111

Providing Full-Service Publishing Services for
Christian Authors, Artists & Organizations: Hardbacks, Paperbacks,
eBooks, Audiobooks, Music & Film

HOLY REBELLION:
Redefining Excellence in Pastoral Ministry
Copyright © 2014 Innovo Publishing
All rights reserved.

Quotations are from THE HOLY BIBLE: NEW INTERNATIONAL VERSION®.
NIV®. Copyright © 1973, 1978, 1984 by International Bible Society. Used by permission of
Zondervan Publishing House. All rights reserved. (American Edition Copyright.)

Library of Congress Control Number: 2014952081
ISBN 13: 978-1-61314-204-2

Cover Design & Interior Layout: Innovo Publishing, LLC

Printed in the United States of America
U.S. Printing History

First Edition: October 2014

I dedicate this book to the Lord for calling me into pastoral ministry and to God's people for loving me unconditionally. I will forever be grateful for the powerful training I received at the Southwestern Baptist Theological Seminary in Fort Worth, Texas.

I also want to dedicate this book to all of the theological institutions that are training and equipping the next generation of Christian leaders to love God's people with excellence.

TABLE OF CONTENTS

FOREWORD

With great sorrow I have watched across the years as some of the most gifted, capable, and even dedicated young pastors have failed miserably in their first pastorate. Worse still, I have watched others fail in every church they served until finally they simply dropped from the ministry. Often I have inquired as to the reason for the failure. Was this young man a poor preacher? No. As a matter of fact, he excelled in preaching. Did he have a moral failure? Oh no. His family life and his integrity seemed to be completely intact. Then what could possibly have gone wrong? Usually the matter is one of some ambiguity at this point. But when all efforts have been exhausted, what usually arises from the discussion is that the young minister failed in his communication of love for the congregation. As a result, he also failed to stimulate the motivation for the work of the Lord as being because "the love of Christ constrains us" (2 Corinthians 5:14). And as a further result of these failures, he also was unable to create a warm spirit of love, which would become the highway of the affection for all the members of the church. Certainly there are other reasons for this failure, but this is the prevalent expression that I hear.

Furthermore, as I recall my early pastorates, I have a sense that I owe those congregations an apology. I was certainly orthodox in my theology. I was even earnest in my desire to produce a church that would honor God. In every pastorate, I fully intended to be sure that it grew until it encompassed everyone in the community if at all possible. My motives were not in error. However, I consider my early pastorates, to a very large degree, as failures for the simple reason that I failed to promote the virtue of love.

Now you will be able to understand why I am particularly jubilant about Kevin Moore's book *Holy Rebellion: Redefining Excellence in Pastoral Ministry.* This book is for the pastor who has comprehended that his assignment in the local church is far greater than simply orthodox and invigorating preaching. He is responsible for how the church looks upon him. He is responsible for how the church views the world, and in so doing he will inadvertently be responsible for how the congregation views him. Kevin Moore is aware that not every church will respond to this kind of pastoral leadership. But he also knows that even a church with a history and background as a "pastor killer" or a self-destructive church can only be healed by the dissemination of the strong medication of genuine Christian love.

Kevin Moore does not speak of a love that amounts to squishy sentimentalism. What he seeks is a deep abiding understanding of agape love—selfless, other-person-oriented, sacrificial, and compassionate love. Moore's years in the pastorate have been years of salient growth. He has seen what love will do, and he has learned to practice it. As these pages dictate, in so doing he has created a congregation that epitomizes the deepest secrets of Christian fellowship.

The fad today is to seek the latest book on leadership. I certainly have no objection to good leadership, and Kevin Moore is as fine a leader as you will see. The problem addressed by Moore in this book is that leadership void of a real grasp and practice of biblical love is no different than leadership that occurs in a Fortune 500 company or any place else in the world. Much may be accomplished, but God's work is never advanced in the same way as that of the world. Kevin Moore knows that getting a handle on what Paul calls, "the more excellent way" is essential. Moore also knows that what such a practice actually unleashes in the church is the most essential single ingredient in the successful growth of the church, namely, torrents of God's love. My counsel to any young preacher is to read the book carefully, opening the ears of your heart. Second, put it to work in your church, but be sure to buckle your seat belt. You are in for the ride of your life. May God be gracious to you as you read and ponder these pages.

Paige Patterson
President, Southwestern Baptist Theological Seminary
Fort Worth, Texas

INTRODUCTION—A CRISIS OF LOVE

How hard can pastoring really be? If I just preach some great sermons, people will be clamoring to come and hear me. Naturally, the church will be bursting at the seams within months of my arrival. The historic growth will probably put us into a position to plant another congregation within three years. None of this wishful thinking became a reality. Truth be told, I was completely overwhelmed at the task of pastoring my first church at the not-so-ripe age of twenty-six. Though I projected confidence, I was secretly questioning whether or not I would survive even a single year. Not long after my arrival, tensions began to rise over an issue within the church leadership. My pathetic attempt to quell the problem among members only ignited the situation further. It was the first of several rookie mistakes that made life difficult at times during my first few years of pastoring. Little did I know at the time, God was using these circumstances to mold and shape me; through every difficulty, God was teaching me how to love His people. The magnificent lesson of love radically transformed my pastoral ministry.

The call to pastor is a call to love God's people. God's powerful, faithful, and overwhelming love for His Bride demands that pastors care for them in the most devoted manner.

While there are many pastors who love their churches sacrificially, not every pastor understands their responsibility in this manner. In fact, unbiblical paradigms for the office of pastor abound today. Although the following examples in no way exhaust the abhorrent models of pastoral ministry, they illustrate a sampling of disturbing trends.

The CEO Pastor

As the chief executive officer, this pastor has all the answers to managing a successful church. His education and experience virtually guarantee his ability to single-handedly lead his struggling congregation toward productivity. Since the CEO pastor knows how to run the church, he must consolidate power so that he can impose and enforce his plan. Committees and other lay leaders in the church are a relentless annoyance. The CEO pastor blithely dismisses the deacon body as obstructionists when they express concern over his aggressive agenda. Without even trying to understand them, this pastor is quick to rid the church of cherished traditions that, in his mind, have contributed to its decline. Since the burden of the ministry rests on his shoulders, he does not have time to trifle with mundane hospital visits or trips to the nursing home. Because the CEO pastor is well-versed in all of the latest theories and methods related to church life, he tends to cajole his unwitting members into fitful seasons of drastic and spasmodic changes in their ministry. As these erratic initiatives fail, the CEO pastor sometimes blames his congregation for not executing his plan properly, when in actuality they were never given adequate time to embrace or even understand the value of their work *or* their efforts. Opposition to his occasional bullish leadership style eventually builds along with a general sense of unrest. The CEO pastor has no patience for a congregation that cannot appreciate his knowledge and leadership abilities. Devoting years to a ministry that refuses to follow him is simply not an option, so he prepares his resume and waits for an opportunity to graciously exit—a career move that he hopes will land him in a bigger church.

The Fashionable Pastor

The fashionable pastor has an unbelievable knack for connecting with unchurched people. With this strength, however, he tends to embrace what he considers to be *en vogue* at the expense of what is biblical. Unencumbered with the "constraints" of biblical exposition, the fashionable pastor mesmerizes the growing crowds with his wit, charm, and ability to weave life lessons into his stories. All too often, he resorts to the sensational in order to draw more and more congregants. The desire to entice guests and prospective members becomes a relentless cycle that demands an ever-increasing amount of resources. Sensational attractions only hold the interest of those who are subsequently offered intensifying levels of awe-inspiring, thrilling entertainment. Shamefully, the goal of relevance and the desire for more people quickly replaces orthodoxy. Although congregations may laud their fashionable pastor, tragedy and crisis will quickly and effortlessly reveal their anemic soul, which is in no way equipped to handle the painful challenges of life. Their underdeveloped knowledge of God through the Scriptures will be no match for the searing pain of tragedy, and death that can strike without warning. Their souls, which are famished for wisdom from God, will agonize hopelessly for a peace that only a disciplined approach to the Word of God could give them. Over time, they will realize that their fashionable pastor did not love them enough to feed them a proper diet of God's Word.

The Rocking Chair Pastor

The rocking chair pastor has been faithful over many years of ministry, but he has suffered enough. Years of pain and trial have taught him to steer away from conflict at all cost. Consequently, he tends to avoid things that might "rock the boat." Knowing the pain and unrest that change can cause, he wastes no time in quelling creative ideas from eager church members. This pastor enthusiastically accepts and defends the status quo. He has mastered the fine art of pacifying the cantankerous and appeasing those who wield power within the church. In fact, he has an uncanny ability to read people and give them exactly what they want, while purposely ignoring what they really need. Although somewhat dizzying at times, the pastor manages to keep everybody roughly moving in the same direction of going nowhere. His preaching is adequate but lacks the fervor that comes from passionately leading his church to pursue God's vision for them. He is eager to preach on sin but not in a way that would indict anyone *or* step on anyone's toes. He caves under pressure, cowers from his deacons, and contends for mediocrity on every level. He skillfully navigates his precious flock away from challenges and gracefully sweeps unpleasant matters under the rug. After a while, his trite and lifeless approach to ministry accelerates the ever-worsening attrition, which the church has grown strangely accustomed to.

The Visiting Scholar

The visiting scholar has a phenomenal intellectual acumen. Every Sunday is a new opportunity for this pastor to tantalize his congregation with fresh insights gleaned from the footnotes of his favorite new systematic theology textbook. His highly developed theological mind prefers to guide his church members through a tangled web of intellectual arguments rather than bore them with the plain teaching of God's Word. He tends to parade his mental prowess because he cannot stand the thought of his sheep not knowing what he knows. He is always well-prepared but not always sensitive to the needs of his sheep. The visiting scholar diligently supports every point of his Sunday morning lectures with a plethora of historical, linguistic, and scientific evidence. For the sake of clarity and with the hope that he will someday publish his manuscripts in a peer-reviewed journal, he painstakingly reads every word of his carefully crafted sermon from the pulpit. Not wanting his sheep to nod off during his message, the visiting scholar ingeniously embeds occasional puffs of erudite humor: a suitable reward for the well-educated among his congregants. He does not find it amusing when people criticize his harshly dogmatic messages on Sunday morning. Nevertheless, he bears with them, knowing that someday they will appreciate the scope and depth of his well-rounded theological education. The visiting scholar cares for his people but refuses any and all interruptions to his rigorous study regimen. Though they are becoming increasingly well-informed about the theological debates of the day, his church is famished for the Word of God. Evangelism, discipleship, and worship struggle underneath his leadership, leaving only a spirit of indifference, which prompts disheartened parishioners to gradually drift away. The "visiting scholar" is a suitable title for him because most recognize that his departure is inevitable.

What's Wrong?

Although the models of ministry above intentionally magnify disturbing tendencies among pastors, hopefully they all illustrate the same point. In addition to deviating from the biblical explanation of the pastoral office, each of them failed miserably to love their church. In different ways, each pastor chose to love himself and ignore the glaring needs of his sheep. The CEO pastor zealously imposed his radical agenda on a church, hoping to advance his career. The fashionable pastor elevated his persona over Christ and maltreated his church by failing to teach them the Word of God. In an attempt to preserve his own well-being, the rocking chair pastor also avoided the difficult path of love, preferring to protect himself at all costs. Shamefully, I have seen myself struggle with some of the tendencies enumerated above. I have been bullish like the CEO pastor and cowardly like the rocking chair pastor. In my heart, I have longed for larger and larger crowds like the fashionable pastor and have been all too eager to flaunt my theological education. I myself have struggled to love God's people the way that God loves them. Excellence in ministry is impossible when the pastor fails to love his church biblically.

It's Time for Holy Rebellion

Can rebellion be holy? Certainly, as long as we rebel against things that God abhors. It's time to rebel against the desire to make ourselves great in pastoral ministry. It's time to rebel against the temptation to lure large crowds with a compromised, unbiblical message. It's time to rebel against the enticement to avoid challenges at all cost. It's time to rebel against the excessively forceful leadership style of those desperate to achieve something for their personal gain. God is calling you to embrace a more excellent paradigm for pastoral leadership.

Unfortunately, our understanding of excellence in ministry is all too often myopic. When we consider excellence, our minds naturally drift toward executing all of our responsibilities in a superior manner. In my ministry, I am constantly looking for excellence. I examine everything from the cleanliness of our facilities to the performance of my staff. While I do not want to minimize the importance of pursuing excellence in these areas, there remains a much more foundational aspect of the concept. Love is the most excellent manner in which to serve your church. Your love for your church will propel you to build up the Body of Christ in ways that bring glory to God. Ultimately, we love because God loves.

God's love for His church extends to every person in your congregation. God loves those who are difficult for you to love. He loves the cranky, the disgruntled, and those who continually try your patience. God loves those who criticize and malign you. God's love for His people is so comprehensive that we cannot even understand it without His divine help. Consider Paul's prayer for the believers in Ephesus: "I pray that out of his glorious riches he may strengthen you with power through his Spirit in your inner being, so that Christ may dwell in your hearts through faith. And I pray that you, being rooted and established in love, may have power, together with all the saints, to grasp how wide and long and high and deep is the love of Christ, and to know this love that surpasses knowledge, that you may be filled to the measure of all the fullness of God" (Ephesians 3:16–19).

We need God's divine power to understand the scope of His love for us. The parameters of God's love are utterly incomprehensible without His divine assistance. God's love for us is "higher than the heavens" (Psalm 108:4). According to Psalm 103:8, the Lord is "compassionate and gracious, slow to anger, abounding in love." God's love is unconditional and unrelenting. The perfect expression of this amazing love is the cross, where He crushed His own son for the world (Isaiah 53:10; John 3:16). We love God because He first loved us (1 John 4:18). Refusing to love your church sacrificially shows contempt for the Father's love for His Son. Excellence in pastoral ministry begins with love for your church.

Another Book on Pastoring?

Why do we need one more book on pastoral ministry when there are so many to choose from? I am so grateful for the volume of literature that empowers pastors to serve their churches with excellence. However, strangely absent from many of them are candid stories of some of their worst blunders. Books that gloss over the painful times in ministry that were self-induced do little to edify pastors who struggle with the consequences of their mistakes. It is not enough to say, "No pastor is perfect" because pastors fail miserably at times. I wish that I was the exception, but unfortunately, I have epitomized imperfection.

While driving down the highway to officiate a graveside service, my mind began to wander. Although I would love to blame my inattention on a combination of the warm Texas sun and the uneventful stretch of highway, the truth of the matter was, I was simply daydreaming. As my mind wandered, I seemed to forget that I was in a funeral procession. Naturally, I became bothered that the cars in front of me were moving in such a dawdling manner. "I'm a busy man, a busy pastor, a busy husband, a father, I don't have time for their lethargic driving." So I stepped on the gas, put my blinker on, and proceeded to pass the slowpokes in front of me. Once I realized what I was doing, I quickly whipped back into the funeral procession and tried to pretend that nothing happened. Let's just say the funeral director noticed! From that day, he began calling me the preacher with the heavy right foot.

I do not intend to paint myself as a glimmering example of the ideal pastor. There is too much pain in the ministry to spend these pages attempting to do that, so it is unlikely that you will read this book and think highly of me. Instead, you will likely thank God that He could even begin to use such a simple person as myself. In so many ways, I fall short of the ideals presented in this book. I intend to consider myself with sober judgment (Romans 12:3) as I lay bare some of the highs and lows of my first years in pastoral ministry. My prayer is that my failures will guard you from making similar mistakes and that my victories will encourage you to greater heights.

I do not write this book because I have an outrageous story to tell, but rather because of the incredible normalcy of my experience, which typifies life in so many churches. Most of the stories I describe took place during my first pastorate, although I include lessons I've learned in my current ministry context as well. In writing this book, I faced the constant difficulty of being descriptive yet not too descriptive, transparent but not exhaustively so. However, the book will be of no use to pastors if it is not an honest reflection of my experiences. My desire is to convey the challenges of ministry and even the humor of certain situations without in any way demeaning God's Bride, the Church of Jesus Christ. I also pray that you will learn to laugh as you struggle through the innumerable awkward and hilarious moments in ministry.

This book does not represent a comprehensive guide to pastoral work or a theology of pastoral ministry. Instead, my aim is to present the lessons God patiently impressed upon me concerning loving my church. You will read in vain for methods that promise fast results. Although this is written primarily to pastors or those aspiring to be pastors, the principles outlined here will be useful to anyone in Christian leadership. This book avoids every trendy gimmick that promises staggering results. On the contrary, I will repeatedly encourage you to take the long, difficult path of love. It is not about what you can accomplish in days, weeks, or months; instead, it is all about what God will do over years as you commit yourself fully to the biblical role of pastor. My aim is to present the foundational principles of pursuing pastoral ministry in the *most excellent way*—through love.

Chapter 1

LOVE YOUR CHURCH BEYOND BARRIERS

"Now to him who is able to do immeasurably more than all we ask or imagine, according to his power that is at work within us, to him be glory in the church and in Christ Jesus throughout all generations, for ever and ever! Amen" (Ephesians 3:20–21).

After completing my master's degree at seminary, I resigned from a large county-seat church where I served as a ministry intern. I had grown so accustomed to the seemingly endless supply of resources. Everything from state-of-the-art sound equipment to the finest instruments was at our disposal. When my pastor gave me the opportunity, it was thrilling to preach in the pristine worship center. I could saunter around the sprawling stage and send my voice soaring into the majestic twelve hundred-seat auditorium. Nevertheless, God called me to pastor a small country church, and I was not prepared for the drastic transition that was about to take place.

Where was I? It felt like the middle of nowhere. Although I had lived nearby for years, I did not even know this little country church existed. I strongly suspected most people in the county didn't know either. A deteriorated sign sat in front of the rather humble sanctuary, which supported a small, white steeple. The sanctuary was adjoined by an even smaller fellowship hall. The interior of the sanctuary, along with the rickety outhouse in the back, made it seem like you were stepping back in time to an era in which the severity of life required simplicity. Like many country churches, a small cemetery filled with gravestones dating back to the late 1800s sat next to the sanctuary. To put it simply, there was nothing alluring about the church's physical appearance. It seemed so small and so insignificant. Is this what God had been preparing me for? Was I to be thrust into obscurity to minister in a place I did not even know existed?

I came face-to-face with my pride that day! Who was I to judge the worth of God's people by such a worldly, unbiblical standard? Who was I to consider this field of ministry inconsequential? God sent His Son, Jesus, to redeem these people, and they were His beautiful Bride. Over time, I learned just how beautiful they were, and they became more precious to me each year I served them. I became amazed at their faithfulness and the manner in which they took care of each other. Their love for each other and ultimately *for me* was truly extraordinary. They modeled honesty, hard work, and perseverance. Since 1883, this congregation had never had a full-time pastor; yet, they unanimously voted to call me to be their first. With great joy and anticipation, I began the important work of leading this loving church. If I was going to pastor them well, I knew that we would have to address the obvious barriers facing us.

It seemed that we were frequently dealing with animals at our church. There were the small ones like the scorpions that loved to frolic near the children and nursery space despite routine pest control. You expect scorpions in the country, but I did not expect to find a kitten hopelessly trapped inside our church wall. Then there were some larger mammals. On occasion, you could smell the distinct scent of what could only be a skunk coming from beneath the church floor, and cows were known to escape their pasture and stroll around our property, leaving fragrant proof of their visits. We also dealt with unwanted pets that people dropped off on our church property. This meant that unless we wanted them to slowly starve to death, somebody had to water, feed, and occasionally take them home. Then there was the dog that howled outside during communion one Sunday morning. Unlike other pets, Lucy followed her owner several miles to church, even crossing four lanes of a busy highway. Our custodian tried to muffle Lucy by chunking leftover donuts at her, but this only encouraged the pint-sized beast. Needless to say it can be distracting to celebrate the Lord's Supper with a dog barking relentlessly outside.

The inadequate facilities proved to be an ongoing challenge. The asbestos shingles on the exterior of the building had been compromised and allowed wasps to fly around the sanctuary in the spring. During one Sunday morning service, I remember a nicely dressed woman getting whacked on the back of the head as her husband attempted to squash the wasp with God's Holy Word. Such a distraction was not quite the catalyst I was hoping for in our worship service. Even worse for me were the days when, after a baptism, I had to change in the room that contained an untold number of decaying wasp carcasses. The roof in the aging worship center leaked the entire time I served there, occasionally prompting mildew, which left a noticeable odor and stain on the carpet after heavy rains. Speaking of foul odors, I should mention the feces that I found on my office floor; my suspicion is that a large varmint crawled into the church through the conveniently located hole in the building's exterior and relieved itself in my study.

Fortunately, at least one rodent demonstrated repentance, in that a mouse made it to the altar before taking his last breath. On days when the mice decided to worship with us, our organist refused to play. I could not blame her. And where you find mice, you can be sure that snakes are not far behind. Thankfully, the snakes that occasionally startled me on my prayer walks around the property never darkened the door of the church. The baptistery leaked, the floor creaked, and the heating and air-conditioning units broke down at the most inconvenient times. The bathrooms had no hot water and were grossly inadequate for even our small congregation. I couldn't blame several of the men who preferred to go out *behind* the outhouse. How in the world was I supposed to do ministry under these conditions?

REALITY CHECK

So you are called to the ministry? Praise God for inviting you into the most rewarding and wonderful job in all of creation! In case you are not yet serving as a pastor, allow me to give you a little "heads-up" about what not to expect in your first church: There will be no billboards giving directions to your location. There will be no television cameras to broadcast your sermons and no media ministry to handle technical matters. You probably won't have IT personnel to build and maintain your church website. In fact, you may not even have a computer, let alone a website. Your worship facility will probably not have a three-tier balcony with a conveniently located elevator. No drama ministry will be at your disposal to creatively illustrate sermon topics. You most likely will not have an incredible office equipped with all of the latest technology to expedite administration and facilitate your study. I strongly doubt that your office will contain a private bathroom or a secluded area where you can study without distraction. You likely will not have a full staff ready to jump into action upon your slightest suggestion. You will be fortunate to have a secretary and a custodian who will listen to you.

Although your deacons may like you, they will need to learn to trust you. Your congregants will gradually get over the "honeymoon" of having a new pastor, and they will be faced with the incredible challenge of loving you unconditionally (1 John 4:20–21). Sometimes, it will seem as though you are the most popular man on the church campus and that you can do no wrong. They will applaud your leadership, adore your sermons, and sing your praises. However, at other times, you will be the subject of their frustration. Now and then you will struggle to understand them, and they will struggle to understand you.

Over time, I came to realize that these people feared debt far more than worshiping in a humble facility. I also learned that they were thankful for what God had provided. They took great care to decorate the sanctuary during the changing of each season. The woman who arranged the flowers did her job with excellence and creativity. They were passionately committed to worship and loved God's Word. They enjoyed sweet times of laughter and joy in that cramped fellowship hall. Not only were they a loving fellowship of believers, they were eager to do ministry in our community and missions around the world. God does not evaluate congregations based upon the caliber of their facilities.

It is one thing, however, to be satisfied and content with what you have, and quite another to become complacent, never attempting to lay a better foundation for the next generation. Is it pleasing to God when we overlook conditions at church that we would never tolerate in our own home? If you had sufficient means to make repairs, would you tolerate rotting window seats and leaking bathtubs? Humble places of worship do not offend God, but complacency does. Inadequate bathrooms and Sunday school space will limit your ability to minister to people. Deficient sound systems, poor handicap access, insufficient signage, and inadequate parking can become a hindrance to your church doing ministry with excellence. Now that I have small children, I understand more than ever the need for exceptional nursery space. I am not going to leave my children in a dirty, cramped room that does not have age-appropriate furnishings. It's not about thinking that my children deserve better, it's about ensuring a safe environment for the most vulnerable. The ministry of the gospel deserves our very best.

For our small congregation, improving our facilities was not about achieving some vain religious ideal or competing with other local churches for prospective members. It was about believing that God had a very special plan for us. Building was about breaking out of a mindset that had bound the church to the past. It was about faith in God's incomprehensible power and love for us. It was also about our love for the next generation that had no attachment to those old buildings. Something had to change!

Love always looks toward the future with hope. We are not satisfied for our children to remain in diapers or never learn to walk. We love them and long for them to go well beyond where they are. As a pastor, loving your congregants means longing for God to spur them farther than anything they have ever experienced. The problem, however, is that pastors become complacent just like their parishioners. After a few squabbles, sometimes pastors resign themselves to accepting the status quo without leading their church past the obstacles. It seems easier to avoid the drama, the pain, the turmoil, and the stress. It's so convenient to cloak our cowardice and lack of faith beneath the shallow religious guise of preserving unity, but churches die when pastors fail to lead them boldly beyond debilitating barriers in ministry. This possibility is not a hypothetical scenario but a reality. Thousands of churches close their doors each year. I wonder how many of those were led by pastors too fearful to lead past the boundaries.

Determine What the Barriers Are

God has a very special plan for your church. Ultimately, it's not about where you want your church to go. It's not about changing the things you want to change or achieving your personal ideal for the church. Instead, pastoring your church has everything to do with where God wants you to go. Without question, there are avenues of obedience that every New Testament church must relentlessly pursue. Beyond these shared expectations, however, lies God's unique mission for your congregation. Pursuing this vision will require addressing the barriers in your ministry.

Upon entering a new ministry situation, you must begin the process of critically evaluating the strengths and weakness of the church's ministry. Notice, it's not about eradicating the things that irritate you but about identifying the things that keep the church from accomplishing what God has called them to do. Any common fool can enter a ministry position and begin recklessly tearing down cherished traditions they find annoying. Your job, however, is to identify unnecessary barriers that hinder meaningful growth. Are their problems with the bylaws, on-going issues with sin, dysfunctional leaders, or doctrinal disputes? Begin the evaluation process quickly, since time has a way of blurring one's acute perception. As you become ingrained into the life of the church, you will become accustomed and perhaps even comfortable with the status quo. A thorough evaluation will help you determine which aspects of the ministry to encourage and which to slowly eliminate over time. Churches can spend inordinate amounts of time, energy, and money on things that yield diminishing returns. With the proper encouragement and leadership, however, stronger areas of the ministry can flourish to even greater heights. The challenge is in identifying the specific roadblocks that hinder the ministry of your church and addressing their removal in a wise manner. This process of critically evaluating your ministry involves more than just identifying obstacles. It is about understanding God's vision for your church.

Begin with Prayer

Loving your congregation through boundaries and into God's vision for your church requires prayer. As I consider God's powerful intervention in my first church, I must say, everything began with prayer. Frankly, it was difficult to see how God was going to answer. I knew that the church would never support borrowing funds from a bank. This meant raising all of the capital in cash—a daunting task for a small, rural church. Our congregation was full of hard-working people, but we were by no means wealthy. Not only did we have to come up with all of the money to construct the new fellowship hall, but we needed to purchase the land as well. Interestingly, an archaic survey of the church property clearly showed that the site where we desired to build originally belonged to the church. Although the church never sold the land, someone was able to acquire it through a technical legality. It was not at all surprising that this could happen in a congregation that had never had a paid secretary or a full-time pastor to properly administrate the affairs of the church. Despite these formidable challenges, we prayed.

I am convinced that God delights to work within the impossible. The Bible is replete with examples of God moving powerfully in the midst of hopeless circumstances. God intentionally chose a young shepherd boy to defeat Goliath. He raised up Gideon, the weakest man from the weakest clan in Manasseh (Judges 6:15), to defeat the foreboding Midianites with a diminished army of only three hundred men. As you trust Him, God will delight to work in your impossible situations as well. Take every one of them to Him in prayer. I began praying for God to give the land to the church even before I accepted the job as their pastor. For seven and a half years, I continued to pray that God would obliterate all the barriers. One by one, God proved faithful to me and to our church. It is, however, not sufficient only to pray. At some point, God expects us to step out in faith.

Take a Step of Faith

We met together in our small fellowship hall during our monthly business meeting to discuss the matter of purchasing the land we needed to build. Not knowing how we would raise the money needed to build the new facility, we stepped out in faith voting unanimously to purchase the land next door. As a pastor, you do not have to be able to see the future or anticipate every nuance of the challenge that lies ahead. However, God does expect you to lead your church in taking steps of faith. God expected Noah to trust Him enough to construct the ark. Imagine how irrational, perhaps even absurd, it must have seemed to build a boat big enough to house so many animals. It's not as though God is extra happy when we finally choose to exercise faith. Without faith it is impossible to please Him (Hebrews 11:6). Consequently, it is impossible for a pastor who refuses to trust God to please Him. Every time I was incited to lead our church toward another step of faith, God demonstrated His faithfulness to us in miraculous ways.

One Monday afternoon while meeting with my prayer partner at the coffee shop an old friend approached. He asked to speak with us after we finished praying. So we took our time, prayed, then went and sat down with the gentleman. He proceeded to ask us about tithing. He was specifically interested in whether or not it was biblically permissible to tithe to a church other than the one he attended. I explained that we ought to primarily support our own church, but that it was not unbiblical to support other ministries as well. He then responded with the loaded question, "What does your church need?" I shared with him that we were in the process of trying to acquire some land next door to build a new educational facility. After hearing the vision of our church, he told me that his secretary would have a check ready for me at his office. The amount was more than we needed to survey and purchase the land. My heart was so full of joy over the gift that we bowed our heads to thank God. From that moment forward, my church members were quick to encourage me to spend copious amounts of time at the coffee shop.

In the world of fund-raising, there are highly specialized and technical methods for success in capital campaigns. Many churches even hire a financial consultant to organize and administrate the effort. In fact,

I went to meet with someone who does this kind of work but eventually decided that a slick, well-orchestrated method of raising money would have offended my church members. It was not a wrong approach, it was just wrong for us. Instead, we simply believed that God would help us to secure the funds necessary to complete the building. After stepping out in faith, an unprecedented amount of money began to pour in. It seemed that people came out of the woodwork to support the building effort. One man who owned an excavation company donated all of the dirt work. Another one of our senior adults donated the lumber and framed the interior. It is amazing what the people of God can do as they trust the Lord, give sacrificially, and do their part!

We made history at our church by tackling such a large project with so few people and so little resources. By God's grace, we built a wonderfully practical facility that met all of our needs for both Sunday school and church fellowships. Not only did we build it debt free, we actually had money left over that we eventually put toward a new worship center. God always seems to bless when His people step out in faith. As time passed, the supplementary fund grew and gave me hope that we could one day tackle the challenge of constructing a more adequate facility for our Sunday morning worship service. It was during this time that God taught me another lesson about loving your people through barriers.

Cast God's Vision for Your Church

Prior to our first building project, there was little convincing to do. In fact, the former pastor had already led them in forming a building committee. Little did I know at the time, but most of the work had been done before I arrived. Building a facility is one thing, but convincing a church of the need is quite another. Although God had blessed us with a wonderful facility that provided space for fellowships and Sunday school classrooms, the dilapidated sanctuary was still a barrier to growth. The congregation had worshiped there for over sixty years. It was built with the salvaged lumber of their previous sanctuary, which had burned down. I knew that the inadequate facility was a genuine hindrance to us reaching the community. The problem was that I seemed to be the only one motivated by the discussion of another construction project. Our former building chairman had suffered a stroke, and the entire enterprise seemed impossible without his leadership. It was during this three-year period that God taught me the discipline of casting vision.

I am not a businessman, a capital fundraiser, or a financier. Looking back, the only thing I did in leading our people was to demonstrate unflinching faith in the God Who created the universe. After praying fervently about something, there comes a time when effective leaders must get others on board. It was not enough for Nehemiah to pray and fast with a broken heart (Nehemiah 1:4–11). If he were going to tackle the colossal task of rebuilding the wall around Jerusalem, he would need others to help him. He enlisted support by casting vision, first to the king (Nehemiah 2:1–8) and then ultimately to his fellow Israelites (Nehemiah 2:11–18). Over the course of months, I did much the same thing.

I relished opportunities to talk individually with church members about the possibility of building a more adequate house of worship. I strategically dreamt aloud to my deacons about a new facility. I can remember walking out into our parking lot, trying to get one of the deacons to envision how the new building might attach to our existing facility. My church members needed their pastor to believe that God could do it. I preached through the book of Haggai, hoping that the story of Israel's reluctance to rebuild the temple would touch their hearts. I have no experience as a draftsman, an architect, or a builder, but I began acquiring floor plans. I called the state convention and talked with their building consultant. I even went so far as to teach myself how to use a computer program so that I could create my own designs. I then selectively showed these plans to several within the church, hoping that God would excite them about the project. As I prayed and cast the vision, God did the work in the hearts of my people, and the entire church was ready to step out in faith again. Faith is every bit as contagious as unbelief!

In faith, we formed another building committee and began the planning phase of the next project. Our capital grew slowly until one rainy Sunday morning when a family from a nearby community donated $100,000 to the building fund. This gift more than doubled what we had saved and finally motivated the church to action. By God's grace, we boldly began this building project months later.

This chapter is not about how to guide your congregation through a building process. Being a loving pastor to your church may have nothing to do with construction. Loving your church means leading them beyond the debilitating barriers. When God makes His will for your congregation clear, I challenge you to lead your people in approaching God with childlike faith. Demonstrate for them what it means to trust God. Dream aloud and challenge others to believe that God can do anything. Seize opportunities to pull people aside and cast God's vision for the future of your church. Let your people hear the vision from the pulpit, during the business meetings, and during corporate prayer services. As you preach through the Bible, teach them to believe in the God Who parted the Red Sea, defeated death, and purchased our salvation. Love your church by saturating them with the vision God has given you. Fix your eyes on God's power and His purpose for your church. Don't ever project a lack of faith to your church members. Rebel against the temptation to sink into the mire of complacency. Don't hide from challenges because of the personal sacrifices you know they will entail. Love your church through the obstacles by challenging them to believe that God can do exceedingly, abundantly beyond all that they could ever ask or imagine (Ephesians 3:20).

REFLECTION QUESTIONS

What barrier(s) does my church need me to love them beyond?
Am I praying for God to move our church beyond these barriers?
What step of faith do I need to lead my church in taking?

Chapter 2

LOVE YOUR CHURCH WITH GOD'S WORD

"Preach the Word; be prepared in season and out of season;
correct, rebuke and encourage—with great patience and careful instruction"
(2 Timothy 4:2).

Faithfully preaching God's Word is the most powerful way to love your church! As I think back over the years of ministry, I can honestly say that everything good in my ministry came from God's Word. God will unify, encourage, strengthen, and bless your church as you preach the Bible. He will humble, convict, rebuke, and train your church in righteousness. The faithful exposition of God's Word will produce results that you could never engender on your own. Nothing you have to say is as powerful as what God has said in the Bible. Faithfully preaching the Scriptures is also a powerful way to demonstrate your devotion to Jesus Christ.

Jesus questioned Peter three times, saying, "Do you truly love me?" (John 21:15–17). Was Jesus uninformed concerning Peter's devotion? Certainly not. Christ was teaching Peter to show his love for God through faithfully feeding his people. God is calling you to demonstrate your love for Him in the same manner. Pastors who find more fashionable things to talk about on Sunday morning not only impoverish their church members but they reveal their lifeless commitment to the Lord Himself. In contrast, consider the following declaration by the psalmist: "I lift up my hands to your commands which I love, and I meditate on your promises" (Psalm 119:48). Surely, God will not esteem pastors who don't value His Word. On a more practical level, if you do not love your church through a powerful pulpit ministry, you will have difficulty leading them.

You may be able to surmount shortcomings in other areas of your job, but you will not likely survive an anemic pulpit ministry. Weak and lifeless sermons are a sure way to incite your church members to question your ability to lead them effectively. Poorly developed, passionless preaching will undermine your credibility as their shepherd. It will encourage your parishioners to ask damaging questions like, "What does our pastor do all week?" or "Why are his sermons so boring?" or "Did our pastor pay attention during his preaching classes in seminary?" People will not respect a pastor who consistently preaches in a confusing, shallow, or rambling manner. If your church members question your competence in the pulpit, they will have difficulty following your leadership. Powerful preaching establishes you as one who is worthy to be followed. Your sermons should inspire your congregation to dig even deeper into God's Word and provoke people to pursue Christ with all their hearts. Your preaching should demonstrate your love for your church. So, how do you love your church with God's Word? As with nearly every other aspect of pastoral ministry, it begins with prayer.

Implore God for Divine Assistance

The power and efficacy of your preaching will correspond directly with that of your prayer life. If your prayer life is anemic, your preaching will be anemic. Loving your church with the Bible requires slaying the self-sufficient streak within you that makes you feel equal to the task of proclaiming the eternal gospel. No matter how long you have been preaching, the magnitude of the responsibility dwarfs your experience, forcing you to cry desperately to the Lord for help. Even your education is not sufficient in and of itself to prepare you for that holy moment when you stand before God's people holding God's Holy Book. No matter how eloquent you are, you have no ability to change a heart of stone to a heart of flesh. Your magnificent oratorical skills are not sufficient to nudge people's hearts even one inch toward their Creator. Even the most thrilling rhetorical masterpieces are powerless to create a thirst for righteousness. Without God's divine assistance, all of your finest efforts will relentlessly fail. With God's help, however, everything changes.

As you pray, the Holy Spirit will enable you to proclaim with all boldness the Word of God. You will be able to preach courageously amidst any and all opposition. As you preach with divine assistance, you will find more delight in what used to be a crippling responsibility. Your church will ignite with a greater passion for God because of it. With His help, the complexities of preaching well will fade behind the all-consuming task of preaching Christ to the people of God. You will gladly give up eloquence for the thrill of preaching with the power of the resurrected Lord. As you proclaim truth with God's favor, God will leverage even what is peculiar about your mode of communication to propel His truth. You will decrease and He will increase!

Cast yourself regularly, fervently, and humbly before God. Beg like a pauper for His help in every stage of your sermon preparation! Perish the thought of standing before God's people with nothing more than your meager ability. Allow the daunting task of preaching to drive you regularly to your knees. Bring every one of your inadequacies to God and pray for His power to be made perfect in your weakness. After praying for God's help, begin interceding for your congregation. Pray for God to exercise His sovereign control over every aspect of the service such that people have ears to hear. Pray that God will sanctify the saved and save the lost. Pray for God to heal marriages and convict people of sin. Pray for God to comfort the broken-hearted and encourage the lonely.

Confess Sin

A pastor friend of mine called the night before his first Easter service at his church. Having completed his sermon preparation, he was not sure what to do with the lingering nervous energy. He asked, "What do I do now?" Without a pause, I responded, "Confess sin." I didn't say this because there was some serious besetting evil in his life but because preaching with power requires a repentant heart. If you want to love your church through preaching, allow God's Word to conform your life to Christ first. Brilliant rhetorical strategies will ring hollow if you have not personally embraced God's Word. Your keen exegetical insights and rousing illustrations will lack conviction if you relate to God's Word only on a professional level. Let your people see a man who has been inalterably pushed, pressed, and driven toward holiness. Let them see a pastor who has been stripped of his pride and self-righteousness by the overwhelming force of God's Word. Nothing is more compelling than a messenger who has been radically transformed by God's Word.

Prepare Sermons with Your Whole Heart

Every now and then, my sermon falls together almost effortlessly. It is a rare and thrilling experience when, in the span of only a few minutes, God sheds almost instantaneous clarity on a biblical passage. This kind of experience, however, is the exception, not the rule. More often, I wrestle for days with the passage I'm studying. I pour over it trying desperately to understand what God is saying. I examine how the passage fits into the immediate literary context, then I study the usage of key terms elsewhere in Scripture, paying careful attention to imagery borrowed from other passages of Scripture. I construct outlines over and over. I write and rewrite my points, fussing endlessly over how to explain, illustrate, and apply the exegetical insights to my flock. I tediously create transition statements between my points so as to create a sense of continuity and movement within the sermon.

With some sermons, I rhetorically craft ways to alleviate the heaviness that I know will develop in the room as I preach the passage. Other weeks, I work hard to create the kind of heaviness that the biblical passage demands. After all of this, I begin the process of practicing the sermon aloud because, with so much at stake on Sunday morning, I am not about to presume that everything will come out naturally in the most engaging manner. I toil over the most compelling way to communicate the various parts of the sermon. I practice the introduction repeatedly, interchanging words, metaphors, and descriptive adjectives. I force myself to articulate my points in different ways so that if I forget a word in the heat of the moment, I have many others to choose from. I work on ways to shock the congregation by driving home the main point of the sermon in a totally unexpected way. As I verbalize the sermon, I rehearse material that must be memorized for maximum impact. I recite Scriptures over and over so that I'm not stumbling over words during the message. Having worked through the sermon aloud, I very often go back to the computer and make further adjustments to my outline. Even after all of this, inadequacies with my sermon outline sometimes emerge Sunday morning before I preach. If I have time, I return, yet again, to the computer to make the final changes. I am constantly searching for the most captivating manner to convey God's perfect Word.

The process that I have just described is repeated each week for every Sunday morning sermon I preach throughout the entire year. This, however, does not include my preparation for Wednesday and Sunday evening sermons. It does not matter how busy, tired, or stressed I am. It does not matter if I am in a bad mood or have a headache. It does not matter how many administrative responsibilities also need my attention. Regardless of how many e-mails I return or meetings I attend, the task of preaching God's Word requires intense exertion.

I consider it a joy and privilege to preach God's Word! I do not ever want to treat the responsibility with contempt through disgraceful and slovenly preparation. God's Word deserves my very best!

Love your church through diligent sermon preparation. Pour over the Scripture passionately and faithfully each week. Study the Bible when you are tired, stressed, discouraged, and busy. Study to the point of exhaustion; rest, and then continue working. Do a thorough exegesis each week. Explore semantically significant aspects of the Hebrew and Greek in the passages you will be preaching. Having completed your own exegetical work, force yourself to read critical commentaries to make sure that you have not missed anything significant from the passage. Don't impoverish your church through taking shortcuts in your sermon preparation, and don't preach other pastors' sermons. Loving your church with God's Word means studying. Tell your secretary that you will need a significant portion of every morning without interruptions. Try to put off responding to e-mails that are not time-sensitive. Turn off your phone, close the door, and sit as a beggar before God's Word.

Be an Expositor

Paul warned Timothy, saying, "For the time will come when men will not put up with sound doctrine. Instead, to suit their own desires, they will gather around them a great number of teachers to say what their itching ears want to hear" (2 Timothy 4:3). In light of the coming reality, which now bears striking resemblance to the evangelical church of the twenty-first century, Paul exhorted Timothy: "In the presence of God and of Christ Jesus, who will judge the living and the dead, and in view of his appearing and his kingdom, I give you this charge: Preach the Word; be prepared in season and out of season; correct, rebuke and encourage—with great patience and careful instruction" (2 Timothy 4:1–2). This command proves difficult in an age driven by entertainment and fascinated with self-help teaching. Many churches respond to the challenge by searching "for what is sensational, entertaining and ego-building,"[1] instead of that which is valuable for teaching, rebuking, correcting, and instructing in righteousness. Albert Mohler claims that the crisis in preaching amounts to "a worldly church proclaiming an increasingly worldly message."[2] How can you proclaim God's truth to people who have gradually allowed secular society to dictate what acceptable preaching is? Respond to the challenge by declaring the Word of God with ever-increasing faithfulness. To neglect this foundational responsibility of the pastoral office is nothing short of insubordination.

Without question, the most effective way to preach the Word of God is through expository sermons. Expository preaching is a method of biblical proclamation wherein the preacher, guided by the Holy Spirit, allows a biblical passage to shape a sermon's style, exposition, illustration, and application in such a way as to present Christ to the people of God. Expository preaching is a logical consequence of the doctrine of inerrancy. There can be no other response to the fact that "all Scripture is God-breathed and is useful for teaching, rebuking, correcting, and training in righteousness" (2 Timothy 3:16). Your opinions, ideas, and general commentary on life are not perfect and do not have power to transform your church. Feed your church members a divine diet. Spread for them a feast of God's eternally perfect truth (Psalm 119:89, 96).

I am consistently amazed at the pain that my church members endure. At any given moment, there are numerous people experiencing unspeakable trials and tribulations. Although I rarely have any personal words of wisdom to alleviate their pain, I know that I can always teach them Scripture, which prompts joy, delight, hope, comfort, and peace (Psalm 119:14, 16, 49, 50, 165). God's Word will cause life, grace, freedom, understanding, and the promise of salvation to flourish in your church (Psalm 119:25, 29, 32, 100, 41). The perfection of God's Word demands that you serve it faithfully to your hungry sheep.

On a more personal level, preaching expository sermons aids your sermon delivery. Right before I was about to preach one Sunday morning, I looked down at my Bible and realized that I had lost my sermon notes. During the time of offering, I frantically rushed out of our sanctuary to go and find the outline I had so carefully prepared. I looked in my Sunday school class, my office, and my truck, but to no avail. My heart raced as I realized that I would have to preach the entire sermon without notes. I concluded that apparently God wanted me to trust Him. So I walked back into the sanctuary, stepped to the pulpit and, after a short time of prayer, preached. Fortunately, because I preach expository sermons, my outline was embedded in the text before me. Although I would have loved to have the supporting verses, quotes, and illustrations I'd prepared, the text gave me everything I needed to preach confidently. Ironically, what would have normally been unnerving turned into a thrilling experience in which I was forced to preach unencumbered by sermon notes.

One of the most wonderful blessings involved with preaching expository sermons to God's people is that it establishes you as their pastor. When you stand week after week to proclaim God's Word to them, you will not have to fight for their respect or compel them to follow you through savvy church politics. They will naturally esteem you as the man who teaches them God's Holy Word. It will cause them to seek your counsel in all areas of their lives. When they see that you are competent with Scripture, they will bring their spiritual questions to you. They will open their hearts to you with some of their deepest worries and problems, thus giving you opportunities to minister to them. In short, they will allow you into their lives as you establish yourself as a man who cares passionately for the things of God. Not only will your parishioners love you, but you will grow to love them as you perform the most nurturing thing a pastor can do—namely, preach the Bible.

Preach Christ

Paul authored thirteen of the twenty-seven books in the New Testament. He was a brilliant church planter and courageous evangelist. Paul loved the Word of God and loved those he ministered to; he persevered in prayer and welcomed the opportunity to suffer for the Lord. The apostle Paul also knew a thing or two about how to pastor God's church effectively. Yet, I am not sure that Paul could get hired as a pastor in today's world. By his own admission, he did not have several of the qualities that churches look for today.

"When I came to you, brothers, I did not come with eloquence or superior wisdom as I proclaimed to you the testimony about God. For I resolved to know nothing while I was with you except Jesus Christ and him crucified. I came to you in weakness and fear, and with much trembling. My message and my preaching were not with wise and persuasive words, but with a demonstration of the Spirit's power, so that your faith might not rest on men's wisdom, but on God's power" (1 Corinthians 2:1–5).

Paul's aim was not to send his audience soaring to new emotional heights, unless you count the fact that his listeners occasionally stoned him. Paul did not have an endless supply of cute, funny stories to warm people's hearts. I have difficulty imagining him beginning each sermon with witty jokes to lighten the mood. Unfortunately, the importance of style over substance is prevalent in today's churches. Many pastors have silently acquiesced to the new expectation and in so doing neglected the most important thing.

Paul also did not come with human wisdom. He is not calling himself a fool; on the contrary, the text suggests that his speech was full of heavenly wisdom. Paul wants the church in Corinth to know, however, that he was not a repository of human wisdom. His sermons were not comprised of homegrown axioms, truisms, and religious principles. Paul would also have abhorred the self-help teaching that pollutes pulpits all across America. Avoid the temptation to turn your sermons into ethical treatises that do nothing more than weigh people down with the guilt that comes from having no ability to live righteously in their own strength.

I think pulpit committees would also have a problem with Paul's "weakness, fear, and trembling." Many congregations want to see their pastors flaunt a remarkable poise as they saunter effortlessly around the stage, and they depend on his charisma to market their brand of church. Although we think of Paul as being inherently courageous, he was not. In fact, in the few times he requests prayer for himself, he asks for courage (Philippians 1:20) so that he might fearlessly proclaim the gospel (Ephesians 6:19–20).

The final strike against the apostle Paul was that he did not come with persuasive words. There is no reason to assume this was false humility, especially since his contemporaries found Paul underwhelming. People thought his writing was "weighty and forceful" and his public speaking "unimpressive" (2 Corinthians 10:10). Then again, Paul was not trying to gain their approval or applause. Though the rhetoric of the day championed a man's ability to sway the masses, he was not trusting in his rhetoric to persuade his audience. Paul did not want people's faith to rest on him. What a refreshing thought, in a day and age where people place so much stock in their pastor's ability to convince, motivate, and rally people to do good things. If your goal as a pastor is to persuade your audience to action, you will instinctively learn to guilt, shame, and scare people into doing things. Whatever short-term "progress" you achieve will eventually die along with people's willpower. Paul placed no stock in eloquence, wisdom, strength, confidence, or persuasive ability. The apostle came with something far more powerful.

Paul trembled before his audience with nothing more than the message of the cross. As Paul preached that message, God unleashed the Holy Spirit in a powerful way. Consider Oswald Chambers' meditation on Paul's conviction.

"Belief in Jesus is a miracle produced only by the effectiveness of redemption, not by impressive speech, nor by wooing and winning, but by the sheer unaided power of God. The creative power of redemption comes through the preaching of the gospel, but never because of the personality of the preacher. . . . Anything that flatters me in my preaching of the gospel will end in making me a traitor to Jesus; I prevent the creative power of His redemption from doing its work."[3]

Saturate your preaching with the message of the cross. Don't attempt to guilt people into praying more; show them how the death of Christ tore the veil, making access to God possible. Don't just tell people to love their spouses; explain to them how the gospel empowers them to love their spouse sacrificially. Don't shame people into tithing; allow the message of God's love to transform people to faithfulness in this area of obedience. Don't tell people to stop sinning; teach them how the work of Christ has freed them from the power of sin. Preach Christ in every sermon. Preach Christ from the Old Testament and preach Christ from the New Testament. Marinate every devotional and Bible study in the life, death, and resurrection of Jesus Christ.

Preach Systematically through Books of the Bible

Your people need the Word of God—all of it. Not just the portions of Scripture you like or the passages that you find particularly interesting. God's people need everything from the legal portions of the Pentateuch to the intricate visions of the apocalypse. Your church needs the imprecatory psalms just as much as they do the psalms of thanksgiving. As a pastor, your job is to proclaim the full counsel of God (Acts 20:27). It is unloving and unwise to ignore vast portions of his perfect Word. Who are you to pick and choose what God's people need to glean here? Do you have the right to say that preaching through Leviticus or 2 Kings is less important than delving into your favorite parables in the New Testament? Can you imagine Moses having the audacity to descend from Mt. Sinai with only the commandments that he found relevant or interesting? What would be unconscionable for Moses has become routine for most pastors. Avoid the conceited and vain ritual of deciding what passages of Scripture you will ignore and simply preach the Bible.

Preaching systematically through the Bible is the only way to combat the increasing biblical illiteracy in Christendom today. Arbitrarily jumping from book to book in order to preach your favorite passages will not foster in your audience a deep understanding of Scripture. It is through apprehending individual books that we are able to grasp the overarching themes of salvation history that tie the Scriptures together. Failing to preach large portions of the Old Testament will impoverish your people's ability to understand critical concepts that appear routinely in the New Testament. How in the world can your church understand the gravity of Christ as our Passover Lamb if you have neglected Exodus 12–15? If your preaching lacks a systematic approach, you will very likely cultivate within your listeners an idiosyncratic approach in their personal study of the Bible. Or, worse, you will train them to ignore the same passages that you ignore from the pulpit! They will learn to disregard passages that are profitable for "teaching rebuking, correcting, and training in righteousness" (2 Timothy 3:16). Preaching systematically through books of the Bible will also help you be a better steward of your time.

I learned early on in the pastorate that Sunday comes relentlessly every week. Preparing three sermons weekly poses a significant challenge for any pastor who is fully devoted to preaching well on a consistent basis. If you habitually spend days trying to figure out what God wants you to preach, you are wasting precious time; time that could be better spent in sermon preparation. Let me make this simple for you; God wants you to preach the Bible. Every single passage is profitable for your church. The entire Bible is capable of thoroughly equipping your church for "every good work" (1 Timothy 3:16). Preaching powerfully every week is a daunting task. Don't waste time. You ought to know early on in the week what passage you will preach the next Sunday. Typically, the more time you have to study, the better the sermon will be. Do not waste precious time. Just preach the Word!

Clearly, the best way to know what you will preach is to be consistently working through a book of the Bible. I am almost always preaching through three books of the Bible: one on Sunday morning, one on Sunday evening, and another on Wednesday night. I may not know the specific topic or the subpoints by Monday morning, but I know roughly which passage I need to work on throughout the course of the upcoming week. This is half of the battle. Once your parishioners grow accustomed to this regimen, they will appreciate knowing what to read in preparation for your sermons. There is virtually no way that your church can adequately prepare themselves for a random and haphazard approach to the Scripture.

Preaching through books of the Bible also saves time in your preparation because you will not have to study the historical context and setting of the passage every time. You will have a very difficult time doing a sufficient amount of historical work in order to deal properly with a new book of the Bible each week. Preaching systematically through books of the Bible causes your knowledge base in a book to grow without having to do all of the leg work week after week. A warning: preaching topically on a regular basis forces the pastor into a position of doing an inadequate job in his sermon preparation. Those who preach topically run the risk of abusing the original intent of Scripture because there are not enough hours in a week to do the necessary amount of research. However, the issue is far more serious than your personal time management.

Preaching systematically through the Bible ensures a proper diet for the people of God. If you refuse to preach systematically through Scripture, you will likely relegate your congregation to the portions of Scripture you prefer or are most comfortable preaching. Your constant attention to the same portions of the Bible will not go very far in countering the biblical illiteracy, which plagues Christians today. Even some who have spent their whole lives in church lack basic biblical knowledge. Sometimes the portions people are most ignorant of correspond to some of the most significant problems in churches today. Yet, it is unlikely that a preacher would randomly choose to preach on spiritual discipline from Matthew 18, Sodom and Gomorrah from Genesis 19, or Paul's prohibition against lawsuits among believers from 1 Corinthians 6. Systematic exposition through the entire Bible will force you to deal with topics that you would otherwise avoid. My commitment to preaching through the book of Malachi required that I deal with God's hatred for divorce. My resolve to preach the book of Leviticus demanded that I addressed sexual ethics. Knowing how unlikely it is for you as a pastor to topically land on painful and uncomfortable subjects, you should commit to a systematic approach that will ensure that you address them. But systematic exposition through books of the Bible is not simply about covering difficult topics. As you preach through books of the Bible, you will routinely encounter wonderful things that you would've otherwise skipped over. Do not impoverish the spiritual diet of your parishioners by addressing only the topics or Scriptures that personally interest you.

In addition to feeding the flock, the personal development of the pastor is at stake. As Walter Kaiser notes, a pastor will not grow if he resigns himself to a small number of well-known passages.[4] Without question, preaching through all of the books of the Bible forces the preacher to journey into different literary genres, requiring different hermeneutical and delivery skills. A systematic approach will force you to study wisdom, prophetic, apocalyptic, and poetic passages in the Scripture. It will also compel you to grow in areas where your natural inclinations and interests do not take you.

Historically speaking, the doctrine of *Sola Scriptura* ("Scripture alone"), which grew out of the Great Reformation, commends systematic biblical exposition. You would do well to listen to the cry of the reformers who pleaded for the centrality of the Bible. Ironically, so many pastors who hail the importance of the Reformation ignore the pillars on which it took place. How can you espouse the doctrine of *Sola Scriptura* while ignoring large portions of Scripture in your preaching?

Some people will balk at the notion of preaching systematically through the Bible, claiming that you are not allowing yourself to be led by the Spirit of God. I think everyone has seen "enlightened" pastors quickly change their sermons on Sunday morning because "God told them to." I don't want to judge their motives, but as a general rule, the pastor does not have to wait to be told what to preach because he has been told already: "Preach the Word, be prepared in season and out of season" (2 Timothy 4:2). Gently remind people who struggle with systematic exposition that you are responsible to proclaim to them the whole counsel of God (Acts 20:27). Like the apostle Paul, God called you to present the Word of God in its fullness (Colossians 1:25). Patiently remind them of Christ's command to teach people to obey everything He commanded (Matthew 28:20). The only way to instruct people in everything God commanded is to preach the entire Bible. Some might claim that you need to be ready to address situations that arise in your church, thus requiring you to remain flexible about your sermons. However, this argument is based on the false premise that God does not address these issues as you pursue a systematic approach. Time and time again, God has proven to me that He will orchestrate the subjects that arise out of the Scriptures in the perfect time to attend to the needs of our church. If, on the other hand, you address a problem in your church on Sunday morning when everyone knows who and what you are talking about, you will harden their hearts and divert attention away from Christ. You must not use the Bible as a weapon against those who cause problems. You cannot play the role of the Holy Spirit.

Critique Your Sermons

The only thing worse than obsessing endlessly over the sermon you preached the day before is ignoring your personal development as a preacher altogether. If you love your church, you will want to make sure that your sermons excel in the most important ways. While you are preaching, however, is not the time to analyze the effectiveness of your sermon. I recommend listening to portions of your sermons about twice a month. If your church has the capability, a video recording is even better. As you watch or listen to your sermon, simply evaluate the quality: Are you preaching too fast or too slow? Is your pronunciation clear? Does the sermon have a sufficient amount of energy? Do you find the sermon engaging or are you bored as you listen? Did you pursue unnecessary "rabbit trails" that diverted from the intent of the biblical passage? Are the key points of the sermon clear? Were you excessively technical or overly simplistic? You can answer these questions and more after only a few minutes of listening to your sermon.

Sometimes, however, you are not the best judge of your sermons. Preachers can at times be fiercely protective of their messages or, on the opposite extreme, harshly critical. Neither extreme will help you improve your preaching. If you find yourself lacking objectivity, I would encourage you to ask your wife what she thinks. Our wives love us and want us to succeed. They have a vested interest in our being the absolute best preachers we can be. That combination of support and honesty will oftentimes produce the most constructive criticism. If you are not married, ask a close friend, a fellow student, or a trusted church member.

If you are struggling with a particular aspect of your preaching, prompt them to pay careful attention to it as they listen to the message. Having critiqued your sermon, make the necessary adjustments then move on.

Rebel against the temptation to be lazy in your sermon preparation. Rebel against the tendency to preach God's Word on your own strength. Pursue excellence! Love your church with God's Word through faithful and passionate biblical exposition. Preach systematically through the Bible knowing that God's Word never returns void (Isaiah 55:10–11).

REFLECTION QUESTIONS

Am I cutting any corners in my sermon preparation?
Am I living in any sin that I am preaching against?
What role does prayer play in my sermon preparation?

Chapter 3

LOVE YOUR CHURCH IN PRAYER

"And pray in the Spirit on all occasions with all kinds of prayers and requests. With this in mind, be alert and always keep on praying for all the saints" *(Ephesians 6:18).*

God has moved so powerfully in my ministry, but I can take credit for nothing. I have simply begged for God to do all the things that I could never do, and He has been so faithful! God has removed barriers, changed hearts, and established unity. God has provided financially in remarkable ways. God has given me strength, fortitude, and courage in my weakness. He has given me boldness to lead His people in new ways. God has overwhelmed my inexperience with His power. God has surprised me with joy time and time again with things that I did not even think to pray for. Your "first business" as a pastor "is to pant after God in prayer."[5] This chapter is not a treatise on the discipline of prayer. Instead, I want to share with you some of the most meaningful ways that God has taught me to love my church in prayer.

Early Morning Prayer

The Lord was gracious to bring a very special custodian into my life. He was a Hispanic gentleman who spoke very little English. He and his wife worked hard every week keeping our church spotlessly clean. Not only was he our custodian, but he was also a pastor of a rapidly growing Hispanic congregation in our local association. One day we ate lunch together and

I asked him to ask God to bless our meal. Although I did not understand what he prayed, I sensed that he was a great man of prayer.

His church was vibrant, strong, and exploding with new members because of his faithfulness to lead them in prayer. Unlike most churches, they didn't just preach about prayer or talk about praying. They didn't just hold prayer meetings in which the bulk of the time was consumed with sharing requests; they actually prayed. They met every Saturday at 5 a.m. to pray. I was intrigued and impressed with them so I began to periodically attend their prayer meeting. Each Saturday morning began with Bible study and then transitioned into prayer. There was nothing flashy or elaborate on these dark mornings. The simplicity of drawing near to God in humility was enough to gather this group of men in fellowship. On the mornings when there was nobody to translate, I simply meditated on Scripture and waited until they were ready to pray. Then the group of men would get on their knees before God and pour out their hearts to Him. It was always a struggle for me to show up at 5 a.m. on my day off, but on one particular morning, I arrived before their pastor did. It so happens that he was late only because they had spent much of the night in prayer and worship. Since none of the other men had keys to the church, we waited outside in the dark until he came. However, his absence did not stop the men. One by one they knelt on the concrete in front of the door of the church and began to pray in the dark.

I thank God for his example because early morning prayer is now one of the driving forces of our ministry at Lamar Baptist Church. On Tuesdays at 6 a.m., I meet with a group of men for the express purpose of prayer. The experience makes my day long and tiring yet always leaves me with remarkable spiritual resilience. We pray for our missionaries who are advancing the gospel around the world. We pray for our ministerial staff and for our deacon body as they strive to serve the Lord with faithfulness. We plead with God to bless all of our ministries and guide us in doing His will. We confess sin on our faces and plead with God to give us wisdom to face the challenges of life. You cannot stand to miss out on the blessings of zealous prayer in your church. Don't just talk about prayer. Love your church enough to lead them in prayer.

Pray Through the Directory

One great way to discipline yourself in prayer is to pray systematically through the church directory. If you are new to the body, this will help you learn people's names, which is the first step to establishing a relationship with them. It will also give you the opportunity to say to people, "I've been praying for you," when you see them. Pray for the parents who are dealing with rebellious teenagers. Pray for the small business owners struggling to make ends meet. Pray for those who are out of work. Pray for those facing debilitating health problems. Pray for those who are depressed. Pray for those who have not been to church in months. Pray for the widows who are still grieving their loss. Pray for those who serve as deacons, ushers, and Sunday school teachers to seek Christ with all of their hearts. Pray for God to teach people to love, give, serve, and walk daily with Him. Pray for people to learn the joy of tithing. Pray for God to heal marriages. Love your church by praying systematically for them by name.

Lead Your Staff in Prayer

You may not have the luxury of serving with other ministerial staff at your church, but if you do, pray with them. I meet with my staff nearly every morning for prayer. This time serves as a constant reminder that without God we cannot do anything of spiritual value. It also helps us develop and maintain a spirit of camaraderie as we bear each other's burdens and target specific needs together. I heard a retired pastor once say that in all of the churches he pastored, he only had one well-functioning staff. Not to say that prayer will eradicate the possibility of difficulties amongst staff members, but without it, you can count on dysfunction. If you want your church members to meet in groups for prayer, your staff had better set the example! Don't let prayer become a mere formality. Model a zealous prayer life for them! It's only in displaying an ardent prayer life that I am comfortable challenging them to pray more fervently. I have told my staff that not only is it "acceptable" for them to spend business hours praying about their specific ministry area, but it is an "expectation." I want to see them with holes in the knees of their pants. I thank God for my staff that has risen to the challenge.

Prayer Walking

Prayer walking is a regular part of my prayer regimen as a pastor. When I am fatigued, sitting and praying is almost impossible for me: I will either fall asleep or daydream. Prayer walking engages my mind and keeps me alert. In addition, I spend an incredible amount of time sitting in my office studying and meeting with people. Getting out of the office is always helpful. Further, the church office can be a bustling place. So, at some point during the day, I quietly retreat by myself to take prayer walks around our campus. Prayer walks encourage a conversational style of prayer that is totally unfettered: I can shout, scream, sing, weep, and know that my Father hears me. I pray through our Family Life Park and the parking lots around our facility. Praying outside fills me with thankfulness as I consider the wonderful creation God gave us to enjoy. I pray all throughout our sanctuary. I walk up and down the stairs into the balcony asking God to grant His Word success as I preach. I pray through all of our hallways and into the foyer. Not only do I find the solitude conducive, but my surroundings prompt me to pray for things that I would not otherwise think about. To me, prayer walking is a tangible sign of my faith that God hears and will answer in His perfect timing.

Fast and Pray

Our country is in peril. Society has determined that homosexuality is morally acceptable, even advantageous for many. Christians continue to lose ground over the biblical definition of marriage. Unfortunately, it's not surprising, since so many Christian marriages crumble all around us. Appalling and senseless acts of violence continue to rattle the relative ease, which so many Americans have come to expect. Yet, for the unborn, the womb is an even more dangerous place. With the rise of biblical illiteracy and apathy toward the things of God, churches have declined and lost their effectiveness. In a desperate attempt to stem the tide of irrelevance, preachers dilute God's Word and offer a banquet of frivolous stories, principles, and truisms from the pulpit. Although the crowds in some churches have increased, the preacher's meaningless fodder proves impotent to effect change in the hearts of believers. Within this cultural context, there is something wrong when pastors are known more for their golf game than for their hunger for Christ. Sunday after Sunday pastors confront the profound darkness with frivolous anecdotes and flippant jokes. So many churches exude the triviality of this world because their pastors epitomize it. The dearth of earnestness among pastors serves as a tacit endorsement of our corrupt world, yet Christ sweetly calls us back to Himself through the neglected biblical disciplines of fasting and prayer (Nehemiah 9:1; Esther 4:3, 9:31; Psalm 35:13, 109:24; Isaiah 58:3f, 6; Jeremiah 36:6, 9; Daniel 9:3; Joel 2:12; Matthew 4:2, 6:16, 18; Mark 2:18; Luke 2:37; Acts 13:2, 14:23).

My first experience with fasting was in college. In a total quandary as to what to do with myself after graduation, I decided to fast and pray for God's direction. To say I was a novice is an understatement because not only had I never fasted before, I had virtually no understanding of it. After briefly studying the concept in Scripture, I began. During this time, God called me in a very compelling manner into vocational ministry. It's not like I had a previous inclination or desire to do so. In fact, up to that point, my only desire was to become a professional musician. Yet God broke through my confusion and gave me a powerful call to go to seminary. Prayer and fasting positions us to hear from God in an unmistakable way. So often in ministry, knowing what to do is half the battle. As you struggle to know and understand God's direction for you or your church, don't disregard the discipline of fasting.

In the pastorate, one of your worst enemies is a prideful sense of self-sufficiency. Fasting enables you to understand your profound weakness and strips away the comfort that keeps you blithely unaware of your desperation before God. You will have no problem seeing the folly of your independent spirit when you fast and pray. Ironically, the awareness of your weakness produces strength as you rely entirely upon the Lord. On one occasion, I arrived at the office and met with a church member who was deeply angry with another person in our congregation. I knew what the person wanted to discuss, and I dreaded the conversation. On that particular day, I had purposed to fast. I'm not going to say that it was painless, but what I can say is that I faced the uncomfortable conversation with a resolve and confidence that was unmistakable. Fasting produces a holy strength that sustains you amidst stressful situations. One of the greatest benefits of fasting is that it encourages the right kind of prayers.

On the eve of a brand-new ministry initiative at church, I purposed to fast and pray. The natural desperation that accompanies fasting prompted me to pray more strategically. Instead of praying for things that would point to my personal success in the venture, I found myself praying for God's will to be done. I began praying for God to do things that I had previously given little or no attention to. This Godward focus also produced resilience from the nagging concerns that would have normally distracted me or stolen my joy. On the day of the new initiative, I witnessed the Lord do far beyond what I had initially thought possible. God caused my church to embrace the new vision and follow my leadership with excitement. But why should I be amazed that God would respond to fasting and prayer in such a spectacular fashion? Throughout biblical history, fasting and prayer preceded mighty acts of God. In the book of Esther, the Lord saved the Jewish people in response to earnest fasting and prayer. God brought about spiritual renewal for Israel in the book of Nehemiah through their fasting and prayer. After Jehoshaphat declared a fast in 2 Chronicles 20, the Lord resoundingly defeated the Moabites and Ammonites. Pastor, you cannot stand to miss out on the blessing of leading your church in fasting and prayer!

I've never been accused of having a robust constitution; it's just the way the Lord made me. If I am not careful to eat regularly, my blood sugar drops, making it difficult for me to think. When I am stressed, I have to be even more vigilant because my appetite subsides, and I just don't think about eating. If only that were all! When my natural resources are depleted, I have to be so careful to eat and drink plenty of fluids. When I don't do this, bad things can happen. Just before my wife delivered our beautiful baby girl, I lost consciousness and hit the floor in the delivery room. The screams coming from the delivery room were not from my wife, but from me. After I regained consciousness, the nurses tended to me, but eventually I had to be admitted to the emergency room because I passed out again and started throwing up. I made such a scene.

I share this embarrassing amount of personal information to make an important point. Despite my profound physical weakness, I can fast without any problems whatsoever! Ironically, I find fasting to be an incredibly nourishing experience. When we resolve to focus unwaveringly on the Lord, we tap into resources that we don't have on our own. Apparently concerned about Jesus' well-being in John 4, the disciples urged Him to eat something. Jesus responded saying, "I have food to eat that you know nothing about . . . my food . . . is to do the will of him who sent me and to finish his work" (John 4:32, 34). It is this context of self-denial that Jesus delivers the beloved statement, "I tell you, open your eyes and look at the fields, they are ripe for the harvest" (John 4:35). In other words, the harvest is waiting for those faithful workers who will deny themselves and serve the Lord out of His divine resources. Pastor, don't neglect the power available to you through fasting and prayer.

Pray All Night

While preaching systematically through the Gospel of Luke, I encountered an intriguing verse that challenged me in a new way. Luke 6:12 says, "In these days he went out to the mountain to pray, and all night he continued in prayer to God." After pondering this verse, I asked myself the simple question, "What in the world would Jesus pray about all night?" It's not as though Jesus had sin to confess or that He lacked God's power. Clearly, Jesus did not struggle to hold on to the promises of Scripture like we do. My questions, however, revealed how poorly I understood the greatness of God and my need for Him. Jesus taught us how to pray, so we should have a good a sense of what He was doing all night on the mountainside.

Jesus taught us to praise our heavenly Father. I can only imagine that He was singing psalms to God, offering thanksgiving, worshiping, adoring, and lavishing love on the Father. We don't understand spending an entire night in prayer because our understanding of God's greatness is so underdeveloped. Yet not even a full night of praise and adoration affords us the time we need to exalt God: it will take an eternity! Those living creatures that surround the throne "day and night" never stop saying, "Holy, holy, holy, is the Lord God Almighty, who was and is, and is to come" (Revelation 4:8). As your knowledge of God increases, so will your capacity to worship Him. We also question the importance of spending an entire night in prayer because we fail to recognize our profound need for God.

Jesus needed His heavenly Father. Jesus faced sickness, fatigue, disappointment, temptation, spiritual attack, and frustration, just like you and I do. Prior to His time spent on the mountain in Luke 6, the religious elite charged Him with blasphemy (Luke 5:21) and criticized Jesus for spending time with sinners (Luke 5:27–30). After picking some grain and healing a man, they also accused Jesus of working on the Sabbath and began plotting against Him (Luke 6:1–2). Perhaps Jesus' night of prayer had less to do with spiritual discipline and more to do with desperation for His heavenly Father. I ask you, when was the last time you walked on water or raised the dead? Do you need your heavenly Father any less than Jesus did?

We vastly underestimate our need for God. Scripture does not have particularly positive things to say about our ability to accomplish things on our own strength. On the contrary, without God we can do nothing (John 15:5). James 4:14 records, "What is your life? You are a mist that appears for a little while and then vanishes." Or in the words of 1 Peter 1:24, "All men are like grass, and all their glory is like the flowers of the field; the grass withers and the flowers fall." We talk about prayer and preach about prayer, but our commitment to prayer will be measured only by our actions. Sometimes our prayer life screams, "God—I don't need you!" What an incredibly arrogant thing to say as a pastor. You have no ability to lead your church without God's help. You can't transform a heart of stone into a heart of flesh. You will never be able to convict the lost or guide the saved. You can't shepherd those in pain and despair through the valley of the shadow of death. "Seek the Lord, all you humble of the land, you who do what he commands" (Zephaniah 2:3).

But some might object to Christ's radical approach, saying, "Wouldn't praying all night simply exhaust Jesus, making it difficult to execute His demanding schedule?" This is a reasonable question to ask for pastors who are already exhausted. Let's return to the context of

Luke 6 and see what Jesus did after spending the entire night in prayer. Directly following this event, Luke says that Jesus ministered to the multitudes that flocked to Him. He healed diseases, cast out demons, and proceeded to proclaim one of the greatest sermons ever preached—the Sermon on the Mount (Luke 6:17–49). After all of this, Jesus traveled to Capernaum, where He healed the centurion's son and raised a man from the dead (Luke 7:1–17). Although I've never cast out a demon or raised the dead, I can say with confidence that traveling and preaching are fatiguing activities. Despite these demanding responsibilities, Jesus ministered with great power to every person. People may exhaust you and drain you, but spending time with the Creator of the universe is what gives you the spiritual vitality to do ministry. As the psalmist says, "The lions may grow weak and hungry, but those who seek the Lord lack no good thing" (Psalm 34:10). Convinced that Jesus had set an example for me, I decided to spend an entire night in prayer.

For several years now, I have chosen to take one or two times per year to pray through the entire night. Typically, my decision stems out of an earnest desire to spend more time with the Lord. Pressing ministry needs and challenges in life also prompt me to action. Sometimes my wife senses when it's time and will encourage me to do it. I'm an avid coffee drinker, so the night always begins with a pot of my favorite coffee, then I start praying. I prayer walk my house and my yard. I pray through Scripture and spend a lot of time journaling prayers. Spending these extended hours in prayer gives me an opportunity to intercede for people and situations that escape my attention during the week. One night, I actually worked my way through portions of our local phone book. The longer and harder I pray, the more convinced I become that God will answer me, which prompts me to pray harder and bigger. It is a wonderful cycle that produces a sweet intimacy with the Lord. Maybe instead of asking, "How could Jesus spend the entire night in prayer?" we should say, "How amazing must it have been for Him to do that!" Fervent prayer is incredible! Am I tired the next day? Certainly. But I am convinced that I accomplish more in one night of prayer than through years of ministering in my own strength.

Spending the entire night in prayer creates an unbelievable spirit of expectation! You walk through life so differently when you patiently pursue Christ in this manner. Instead of waiting with dread for an upsetting phone call or e-mail, you literally can't wait to see how God is going to answer. I also find that He gives me an incredible tenacity to persevere through insurmountable challenges. As I pray, God fills me with hope and strength to obey. During one overnight session, I prayed specifically for wisdom about an important decision that I had to make as a pastor. The stakes were simply too high to make the wrong move. I believe with all of my heart that God answered that prayer, giving me amazing clarity on the issue—not only for me, but He brought other leaders in our church to the same conclusion. After another session, I witnessed God work miraculously in the life of someone I had never met before. I don't really know how to describe it other than to say that God completely overwhelmed this person with His Holy Spirit. After a brief interaction, this person nearly crumbled in desperation for God. I can assure you that this does not happen to me very often, but it happened after spending the night crying out fervently to God. This stranger saw Christ in me and longed to be closer to Him. The encounter left me completely amazed with the Lord. God manifests His presence and power through us as we cry out to Him with all of our might.

Pastor, have you ever prayed to the point of physical exhaustion? Have you ever cried out to Him so fervently that your throat began to hurt? Does your preaching demonstrate a power that can only come from the living God? Don't just talk about prayer; lead your church in desperate pursuit of Him. Rebel against the temptation to do ministry in your strength. The seriousness of your responsibilities as a pastor demands that you seek the face of God with all of your heart.

Join the mighty chorus of believers who have cried out in desperation for God. Follow the example of Christ Who travailed greatly in prayer. Love your church excellently in prayer!

REFLECTION QUESTIONS

Am I disciplined in my prayer life?
Am I leading others in my church toward a disciplined prayer life?
In what areas does my prayer life need to mature?

Chapter 4

LOVE YOUR CHURCH THROUGH VISITATION

*"Religion that God our Father accepts as pure and faultless is this:
to look after orphans and widows in their distress"*
(James 1:27).

What does your vision, your faith, or your administrative skill accomplish if the church is not fully convinced that you love them? Your finest oratory will fall on deaf ears if you have not convincingly established your love for them. However, when they know that your love for them is genuine, they will listen intently to your sermons. Visiting your church members communicates love because it requires spending your most precious commodity—your time. As life becomes increasingly busy, time becomes more and more precious. Devoting time to your church members on a regular basis communicates how important they are to you. Faithfully visiting your flock will go a long way in establishing you as their pastor.

Visit the Widows and Widowers

She was one of a kind! Aunt Jettie was the oldest widow in our small country church, and she expected me to visit her every week. Over the years, I spent an untold number of hours listening to her reminisce about the good old days on the farm. Over and over she recounted the same stories. She loved to talk about Ezra, the love of her life, who had gone to be with the Lord decades ago. With joy, she reminisced about milking cows, canning, and killing snakes in the barn with her hoe. She liked the simplicity of her life on the farm and was mostly ambivalent about getting electricity in her simple farmhouse. I say mostly, because she couldn't help but cherish the convenience of a washer. In her later years, she cherished visitors, going to church, and watching Wheel of Fortune.

She knew my cell phone number by heart and was not afraid to use it if I did not show up on time or if she needed me to open her prune juice. In her mind, there was no quota on the number of times she could call if I was on vacation and failed to answer the phone. She would have been horrified to learn that I knew she loved to dip tobacco and that she routinely faked her stumbling so that I might fuss over her. She wanted me to perceive her as the frailest widow in the church. If I voiced concern for another widow in the congregation, she would quickly retort with how surprisingly "stout" they were, in an effort to regain my attention.

For decades, Aunt Jettie delighted in feeding her preacher on Sundays. However, her health would not allow her to perform this act of love anymore, so she insisted on serving me Cheetos and coffee during every visit. I ate the Cheetos for a while, but I grew weary of them and started feeding them mainly to my dog when he accompanied me. The Cheetos were most undesirable when they became stale—few things are worse. Every now and then, she would offer me a cake that someone baked for her. If I refused the cake, she became frustrated, but if I ate too much she told other church members that I came and "pigged out" on her food. She reported to others what we talked about and how long I stayed; anything less than one hour was simply unacceptable.

I could always count on Jettie to give me her unfettered critique of my job as a pastor. Though never unkind, I always knew when my decisions did not meet with her approval. Aunt Jettie was also very opinionated about my Sunday morning attire. Not only did she want her preacher wearing a suit and tie, she wanted the shirt to be white. Since her only outing all week was Sunday morning worship, my visits meant a great deal to her. She had outlived almost her entire family, so she depended greatly on her church family. I know that she loved me and I know that she loved the Lord. She faithfully read her Bible and came to church every Sunday when she was able. Her one abiding irritation was that she was not yet with the Lord in heaven. Aunt Jettie went to see the Lord after experiencing complications from a broken hip. The phone rang well after midnight with the news of her passing, so I got in my truck and drove to the nursing home one last time. I suppose there wasn't any purpose in my being there, but it was what I had always done and it seemed right. I will never regret the countless hours I spent visiting Aunt Jettie; loving her was "pure and faultless."

Visit People in Their Homes

So many pastors are completely detached from the pain that their flock goes through. Those experiencing emotional turmoil rarely divulge their problems at church for fear of shame or reproach. Consequently, many parishioners linger in pain for lack of spiritual guidance. Visiting your flock enables you to apply the truth of God in an environment where they are most receptive. Not only does it benefit your sheep, it will benefit you as a preacher. As you spend time with them, you will know intuitively how to explain, illustrate, and apply the Word of God to their lives. Sharing their sorrow and joy enables you to preach with a measure of depth and relevance that you could never acquire from the most in-depth research.

Despite the fact that there have never been greater demands on my time, I go visiting nearly every Monday afternoon with one of my deacons. It has taken almost two years to visit systematically just the senior adults who are enrolled in Sunday school. Knowing that it may be years before we return to a person's house, we take our time. I love getting to know my people over coffee. There is simply not enough time on Sunday morning to build relationships. Spending time with them in their living rooms gives me time to ask them questions, read them Scripture, and pray for them. I am humbled by the example of Paul W. Powell, who began the discipline of visiting the home of every member in his first pastorate. He then maintained the practice even when he had as many as four hundred families in his church.[6] Some of your church members will need regular attention and others require much less. As you build relationships, God will give you discernment on how to minister to each of them.

On more than one occasion, I learned the value of calling people before I went to visit them. In the summer, it becomes excruciatingly hot in North Texas. Apparently, walking around the house without a top is an alternative to turning on the air conditioner. Although this may seem logical for some, I was shocked that one of our elderly widows came to the door without her blouse. It was difficult to pretend the awkward moment never happened when both of us were certain that it did. Despite the occasional awkward moments, I still prefer unannounced visits because it seems to create a more natural interaction. If people know that I am coming, they clean, wash, and prepare to entertain me. However, if I surprise them—barring any indecent exposure—it often creates open times of fellowship devoid of pretense. You should use discretion and good common sense, though, because most young adults do not appreciate unexpected guests.

I regularly went unannounced to see an eighty-five-year-old widower in our church who had been bound to a wheelchair for years. He delighted to see me each time I came. We talked about church, sports, and the good old days when he was a dairy farmer. I was thankful that he encouraged me to buy milk at Braum's instead of buying a Jersey cow. I did most of the talking since his stroke damaged his ability to speak, but other times we just looked out at the pasture. I frequently read him Scripture since he could no longer read on his own, and I always prayed for him at the conclusion of each visit. After almost every prayer, he would cry. At times, uncontrollably. I never knew what made him cry, but I knew that my coming meant the world to him. I visited him until he died. It was pure and faultless.

Visit the Lost

Every now and then visitation presents the ideal opportunity to share the message of the gospel. Whether they are relatives or friends of church members, I always welcome the opportunity to visit people who may need to hear the Good News about Jesus. Don't be shy with the gospel! I can remember telling one man in his barn, "I'm here today because there are people who love you and are concerned about your spiritual well-being." On another occasion, I went to visit a man who turned out to be one of the angriest people I have ever met. After he spewed his vitriol about everything ranging from the government to the church, I had an incredible opportunity to talk about the importance of forgiving others and being forgiven by God. Currently, most of our ministerial staff members take turns leading an evangelistic outreach program on Sunday afternoons. The initiative consistently presents numerous opportunities to share the gospel. Just in case you have not heard, visitation is not dead! The Internet and social networking sites will never replace the need for Christians to do the work of evangelism in the community.

Visit in Crisis

It was one of my first Sundays on the job. The daughter of one of our faithful church members had been critically injured in a car accident. I remember getting the phone call, and at first I responded in the way that I always had: "I'm so sorry to hear that. Okay, I will be praying." Then it dawned on me, *their family needed me.* Actually, it was not that they needed me; they needed the pastor, the man whom God had called to the sacred office. They needed him to come and reflect the perfect love of Jesus Christ, the Good Shepherd. They needed their pastor to pray and encourage them. That Sunday morning I rushed fifty miles to the hospital and another fifty miles back to the church, making it back just in time to preach. I can't say that I did anything noteworthy at the hospital. There weren't any grand prayers or inspiring devotionals. I certainly did not save the day, but I was there and he never forgot it. That small sacrifice meant the world to him and paved the way for a deep respect that I could have never earned through the finest oratory.

Probably the most difficult house call I have ever made was to the house of man who committed suicide by a gunshot wound to the head. Words cannot express the despair that ripped through his family. There was nothing I could say to his mother or to the rest of the family reeling with shock. The moment did not require a sermon, just my presence. My presence reminded the family that they could turn to Christ and to our loving church that would do anything to support them. The family always knew I would show up when life took unexpected turns. They knew because I went to the karate matches, the rodeos, and to the emergency room when one of them had been injured by a horse. They knew I would come because I came even when nothing was happening, just to see them and talk to them. The bonds forged during times of crisis are unbreakable. To this day, I am confident that this sweet family would do anything for me.

Unfortunately, suicide is a reality in the ministry. Spending time at their house after the suicide taught me a valuable lesson. Always take suicide threats seriously. Although nobody received warning about this man's intentions, I know now the horror of such an occasion. When somebody calls you and informs you about a possible suicide, drop everything you are doing and go. However, I would caution you to always tell somebody where you are going and never go alone. You never know what the situation will be when you show up to the person's house. For all you know, the suicidal individual may be inebriated and holding a shotgun. If you are not cautious, you may be the casualty. Depending upon the circumstances, it may be appropriate to simply call the police.

Visit People in the Hospital

Years ago, I remember being told by a professor who had no pastoral experience that pastors need to learn to send lay people in church to do their hospital visits for them. Such advice quickly revealed ignorance concerning the dynamics in smaller churches. Dispatching someone to the bedside of a sick or dying church member instead of going yourself is an impeachable offense that you will not soon recover from, especially since the person that you failed to visit may be related to a dozen others in your church. People long to see their pastor. Your presence calms them, cheers them, and gives them hope. Mobilize your deacons, staff, and laypeople to share the work of the ministry, but don't neglect your sheep when they need their pastor.

Take time to be with your people when they are going through difficult circumstances. They will never forget that you visited them when they were about to go into surgery. They will always remember the time you drove four hours just to be with them in their time of need. Your trips to the hospital, the jail, and the nursing home will not be wasted. Bonding can literally happen overnight when you have been by somebody's side in the midst of a storm. They will trust you sooner and respect you as their pastor if you shepherd them through the dark times.

Visit Others as You Would Like to Be Visited

Have you ever stopped to consider the fact that one of these days you may be desperate for a visit from your pastor? Like everybody else, you will grow old and eventually retire from the pastorate. You may outlive many of your pastor friends and find yourself spending long afternoons all alone. So many Christians will have an extensive list of reasons for why they don't have time to come and see you. It won't matter how many people you visited or how large your churches were. Most will not care if you authored several books or if you had a successful radio program. Hopefully, you will have a godly pastor who loves his sheep enough to come and spend a little time with you. Maybe your eyesight will be so poor that you will want him to read the Scriptures to you. You will want him to encourage you and remind you of all of the things you faithfully preached. You will hope that he's not too busy at the church office to have one simple cup of coffee with you. Pastor, the Bible says, "So in everything, do to others what you would have them do to you, for this sums up the Law and the Prophets" (Matthew 7:12). You have no control over how your pastor will minister to you in your old age, but you can resolve to love your sheep the way you want to be loved. Love your church through regular and faithful visitation.

Visitation Sweetens the Journey

After spending much time with my church members, the ministry just grew sweeter and sweeter. When you truly know a person, you know how to minister to them. You know if they want to laugh and joke or if they're too wounded to be teased. Even more, you know how to minister to their family after they die. It was a sad day when our church said good-bye to Miss Lawanda. She had been a faithful church member and the wife of one of my deacons. Preaching at her funeral did not feel like a ministry assignment or a speaking engagement because she was my friend. After she died, I sat down with her family to hear their stories and memories about her. But frankly, I already knew what I was going to say about her life, her example, and her walk with the Lord because I knew her. I knew about her life, her hobbies, and her love for her family. I knew the silly jokes she loved to tell me over and over. I knew her dog's name and how she took her coffee (two Sweet'N Low's and some ice). I knew how she loved to take day trips up to Oklahoma to gamble and that she always had her hair fixed at the beauty shop on Friday with her best friend. I knew her neighbor was Church of Christ and that she loved to play her bowling game on the computer. I knew her sons and her grandsons. These were memories to cherish fondly.

Rebel against being distant and emotionally detached from your church members. People will not follow your bold vision if you have been cold and withdrawn. They will never listen to your correction if you have failed to demonstrate your love for them. Your ability to comfort, disciple, and encourage hinges on establishing genuine relationships with them. Even more compelling than these reasons, however, is the fact that spending time with your people through regular visitation sweetens the journey. Through regular visitation, you will establish relationships that will last a lifetime. Don't miss out on the incredible blessing of visiting your sheep.

REFLECTION QUESTIONS

Do my church members know that I want to spend time with them?
How can I incorporate systematic visitation into my ministry schedule?
How can I share the visitation responsibility with other leaders in my church?

Chapter 5

LOVE YOUR CHURCH DURING CHANGE

"If you really change your ways and your actions and deal with each other justly, if you do not oppress the alien, the fatherless or the widow and do not shed innocent blood in this place, and if you do not follow other gods to your own harm, then I will let you live in this place, in the land I gave your forefathers for ever and ever"
(Jeremiah 7:5–7).

I was approached by a student at seminary who shared his desire to take a small congregation and help them grow and change over his tenure as pastor. I turned to him, smiled, and said, "That is exactly what your church members will say about you." The irony caught him off guard. Young pastors see their churches as desperate sheep longing for wisdom, help, and personal growth. Established churches also consider their young, burgeoning pastor in need of wisdom, help, and personal growth. Frankly, it is an arrogant and dangerous posture to take. It is incredibly condescending to think or act like you have all of the answers after a few years of Bible college or seminary. I went on to explain to the student that God had an agenda for him as a pastor, namely to break and humble him. Introducing change into your church is one of the most difficult things you can do as a pastor. It is a path filled with potential land mines for you and for your congregation. Learn to love your church during times of change.

An Agenda for Change

One of the worst things you can do as a pastor is to enter your new church with a rigid agenda for change. Honestly, when you are new to a church, you do not know what needs to change. You may think you know, but most likely, you don't! It takes time to identify the dynamics of a church. For example, you might recognize that somebody has a bad attitude, but it takes time to discover the root of it. Or you may find that the church has peculiar ways of doing something. However, to change their mode of operation without first understanding why they operate that way is foolish. You will not learn what will work in your church until you build relationships with your people. Things that appear to be significant problems in themselves may in actuality only be symptoms of far more systemic issues. In the same way, the things that initially appear to be problems may not be at all. Identifying the root causes is not something that you can do overnight.

Pastors who enter their churches with an aggressive agenda for change also err because they are after the kind of change that does not matter! Some pastors will "go to the mat" over the style of music. You will not endear yourself by demanding your personal penchants in worship music. Those who agree with you will leverage your influence to get their way, and those who disagree with you will end up despising you over something that is truly inconsequential. Seriously, can you honestly say that God will support you as you introduce strife to your church over a musical preference? Other pastors bring a dogmatic argument for small-group ministry or the adoption of the latest method in church growth. At the end of the day, all of these issues are tertiary or secondary at best. Do not alienate yourself from your sheep by pursuing mere cosmetic changes to the ministry. These surface alterations will make your congregants skeptical of your leadership when they begin to see how the shallow changes fail to produce meaningful results. These superficial adjustments will most likely disappear the minute you are gone. It is God's agenda for change that matters, not yours! Your job is not to manipulate your church into doing what you want them to do; it is to lead your church in submitting to Christ.

If you want to pursue an agenda for change, be sure that it is God's. Make no mistake; he wants to bring about change in your church, just not the superficial kind so many pastors are obsessed with. God wants to correct the disobedience in your church. God wants to transform the worldly nature of your church. God wants to soften the calloused hearts of the people. God wants to turn the hearts of His children to their heavenly Father. God wants to annihilate their lust, greed, pride, addictions, and selfishness. God wants to revolutionize the way they treat one another. God wants to alter the way they treat their spouses. God desires change in your church just as He desires *change in you*. God wants to abolish your self-reliance, spiritual lethargy, and prideful spirit. He wants to transform your heart and your mind so that you reflect Jesus Christ. God wants to replace your desire for recognition with a longing to take up your cross daily. Do not waste valuable leadership capital and energy working toward change that does not matter. Having addressed the most important kind, let's turn our attention to how to initiate this change in a church.

Agents for Change

Contrary to popular belief, the agents of change in your church are not young people. Actually, they can fight just as passionately for a cherished tradition as any older person can. In fact, almost anyone can be an obstacle to positive change in your church. It is, therefore, unreasonable to base your hopes for change on attracting younger families to your congregation! Likewise, contemporary music is not an agent for change. Contemporary music can be boring, drab, and lifeless, just like traditional music at times. A particular style of music is not an agent for positive change. Some churches think they can effect positive change by hiring a young, charismatic preacher. This foolish criterion alienates experienced pastors who are called of God and empowered by the Holy Spirit and glorifies inexperienced ministers who may have nothing more than a favorable persona. No church will prosper when fueled only by the strength of the pastor's personality, no matter how likable. Having surveyed some of the most prominent examples of superficiality, let us turn our attention to the real agents of change.

The Word of God is the most powerful agent of change in your church! Paul recognized this reality and boldly proclaimed, "I am not ashamed of the gospel, because it is the power of God for the salvation of everyone who believes . . ." (Romans 1:16). God, by the power and efficacy of His Word, changes the eternal destiny of sinners. Those who were dead in their transgressions and sins can find salvation in the message of the gospel. God rescues the wicked from the dominion of death and darkness through His powerful Word. God created the world, raised the dead, and built His church in the midst of intense persecution, all by His Word. God's Word accomplishes the most profound spiritual change imaginable. However, His Word effects more than the changes of the heart. Through the preaching of Haggai and Zechariah, God mobilized the disgraced nation of Israel toward rebuilding the temple in Jerusalem. God's Word is powerful! Don't be so obtuse as to think that musical styles, buildings, and charismatic leaders are sufficient replacements for the transformative power of God's Word.

While the pastor is not the principal change agent, God does use pastors to facilitate meaningful change in churches. If we want God to use us to facilitate change, our ministry must reflect a disciplined zeal for the fundamentals of pastoral ministry. Every job entails proficiency in executing a certain number of tasks. For example, a police officer must understand the state laws that govern the citizens he or she is sworn to protect. They must likewise have an acute understanding of their own rules, protocols, and procedures. Officers must know how to safely and accurately discharge the weapons at their disposal. It is unconscionable that a police officer could effectively serve and protect citizens without these prerequisites. Similarly, pastors can only lead their church toward positive spiritual change when they commit themselves in a disciplined and faithful manner to the fundamentals of pastoral ministry. It cannot be accomplished with only a blithe commitment to prayer, discipleship, evangelism, visitation, and expository preaching. "One of the greatest sins in the ministry today is indiscipline . . ."[7] At some point, conviction then leads lazy pastors to attempt herculean goals that their untrained mind and lethargic spirit cannot pursue past a few days. The flexible schedule of some ministers contributes to a slothful unwillingness to work in a disciplined manner. Pastors rarely have a regular system of accountability in place. Yet, like every believer, they will "appear before the judgment seat of Christ, that each one may receive what is due him for the things done while in the body, whether good or bad" (2 Corinthians 5:10).

Nothing can undermine your ability to lead your church through seasons of change more than problems with sin. According to 1 Timothy 3:2, the "overseer must be above reproach." Years ago, I assisted a seminary professor who, for the sake of preserving class time, instructed his students to complete quizzes at home. As the grader, I noticed that one particular student had difficulty with Hebrew assignments while in class yet performed brilliantly on the take-home quizzes. Knowing that this student was very likely cheating, I informed the professor, who then confronted the student. To our surprise, the student, at the beginning of our next session, confessed his sin to the entire class. It does not surprise me that students cheat on tests. Seminaries routinely deal with plagiarism and other ethics violations. It was, however, disturbing that he was serving as a pastor at the time. Pastors must overcome the temptation to wander from a close relationship with God, understanding that it leads to the worst hypocrisy.[8] Concerning sin in the lives of pastors, Richard Baxter eloquently articulates the following:

> O what a heinous thing is it in us, to study how to disgrace sin to the utmost, and make it as odious in the eyes of our people as we can, and when we have done, to live in it, and secretly cherish that which we publicly disgrace! What vile hypocrisy is it, to make our daily work to cry it down, and yet to keep to it; to call it publicly all naught, and privately make it our bed-fellow and companion.[9]

Paul seems to have this same very concern in mind when he writes, "I do not run like a man running aimlessly; I do not fight like a man beating the air. No, I beat my body and make it my slave so that after I have preached to others, I myself will not be disqualified for the prize" (1 Corinthians 9:26–27). If you cannot say, "follow me as I follow Christ," your life lacks the personal holiness necessary to lead your church toward positive spiritual change. Not only will you be unable to effect anything positive, your example will prove detrimental to the overall spiritual health of the church. We see over and over in the Old Testament how the wickedness of Israel's leaders led to rebellion among the nation as a whole. Don't become a stumbling block to the process of sanctification in the lives of your church members.

Having considered the most important kind of change that God is aiming for, let's turn our attention to the more common issues related to changing various aspects of the ministry at your church. As you work toward spiritual transformation in the lives of your church members, you will also bear the responsibility of facilitating other kinds of changes to how your church does ministry. Here are a few of the lessons that God has taught me about loving my church during seasons of change.

The Time for Change

The right thing at the wrong time is the wrong thing, and the wrong thing at the wrong time is the wrong thing. Only the right thing at the right time is the right thing. Indeed, God has made all things beautiful, in its time (Ecclesiastes 3:11). You have probably heard it said that it is unwise to work toward changing your church unless you have been their pastor for at least one year. The basic logic is that people will follow you anywhere once you have had the privilege of ministering to them. While I agree with the axiom in principle, I want to suggest that the time frame for this kind of trust to develop is naively optimistic. The pastor who treats his one-year anniversary at the church as a license to change whatever he wants is in for a terrible shock. I can only imagine how that encounter with the church might go . . .

"My dear church, you have been so blessed by my wise pastoral leadership for a full twelve months. In case you were wondering, that's 52 weeks, 365 days, 8,760 hours, 525,600 minutes, and over 31 million seconds. Aside from eight hours of sleep each night and my vacation days, in which I was resting from my arduous pastoral duties, I have led you faithfully. The understanding and wisdom that I have gleaned during this time surprises even me. I'm sure that we can all agree that you can trust me implicitly to change anything I deem necessary going forward."

Ministering to a church for twelve months does not automatically grant you any kind of sovereignty. I would caution you not to adopt any arbitrary length of time as a license to introduce drastic changes to the operation of your church. A year of hard work may seem like a long time to you, but remember there may be some in your congregation who have been members for over half of a century! In a number of churches, a year is barely long enough to learn everybody's name. Sometimes it takes years to facilitate positive change in your church. A loving pastor will wait for the right time. I have learned that when God is ready, He will create the environment in which the congregation will receive it well. If you are patient to wait for the right time, God will very often create the consensus you need to initiate the change. Even better, sometimes God will leave you out of the loop by prompting church members to raise the need for change. Don't gripe or complain to church members about your desire to change something. Instead, pour out your heart to God and allow Him to create the conditions where the change will be received well.

Not Too Fast

One night, I stayed up till the early hours of the morning praying and journaling over the importance of planting churches. I sensed God calling me to support this ministry in some manner. Not long after this, a friend of mine approached me with the opportunity for our congregation to sponsor his new church plant. It did not take me long to begin to position our church to take on the responsibility. Since we did not have much time to enter into this covenant relationship with the new congregation, I scheduled a vote to take place after worship one Sunday morning. Dissension quickly built in our church because my sweet flock did not understand the responsibility or the implications of sponsoring a church plant. What kind of financial obligation were we agreeing to? Would our congregation be liable or responsible for problems with their ministry? What was the mechanism for holding their pastor accountable? I simply did not take enough time to answer their questions.

When the day of the vote came around, we had nothing short of a showdown. The director of missions from our association and I answered their questions but did not assuage their concerns. After intense discussion, I called for a vote. Surprisingly, the motion to sponsor this new church plant was adopted by a two-thirds margin. Although I had succeeded in getting the measure passed, I failed because our congregation never fully supported the project. After approximately a year, I initiated ending the sponsorship agreement because it continued to be a point of contention in our fellowship. To make matters worse, the church plant closed their doors about two years later. What I failed to realize was that this church, since 1883, had never planted another, and that bringing them to this new, exciting level of obedience would take time. I should have preached about church planting from the pulpit, explained it systematically to the deacons, and worked to build consensus among other key leaders. I should have led the church in praying about this initiative for as long as it took. The Bible says, "It is not good to have zeal without knowledge nor be hasty and miss the way" (Proverbs 19:2). My zeal and haste overcame my love for them and caused me to miss the way. If you have succeeded in altering some aspect of your ministry but have not brought your church to the point of embracing and supporting it, you have failed.

Slow is not always bad because meaningful things take time. The Bible teaches that, "A man's wisdom gives him patience" (Proverbs 19:11). If you are a wise and loving pastor, time is your friend. The longer you are there, the more credibility you will have to initiate meaningful change in your church. Time gives you opportunities to build relationships with people outside of formal business meetings. Prompting change is not about telling people what needs to happen. You don't like to be told what to do, so don't expect your church to like it either. Instead of demanding your way, share the burdens that God has placed on your heart. Give them time to cultivate similar desires for their future. After they embrace the vision, they will very likely come alongside you and either improve your plans or help them succeed. This approach shows a gentle love and respect for people who have legitimate reasons for thinking differently than you. If I want my children to follow me when we are about to walk through a parking lot, usually all I have to do is extend my hand toward them. Without me having to say a word, they instinctively take hold of my hand and follow me. My children do not question my love, my care, or my guidance; they simply follow me. Your goal as a pastor is to love your church to the place where all you have to do is "reach out your hand." It is important to note, however, that a pastor can also err in moving too slowly.

Not Too Slow

Every now and then God brings about circumstances that convince the entire congregation that something must happen. When this occurs, you should seize the opportunity to move forward while thanking God for bringing unity on the matter. On one occasion during a routine piano tuning, the technician was unable to properly tune our old, worn-out piano. He told us that the instrument would soon develop problems with several of its strings. While this may seem to be bad news, I immediately became excited at the prospect of purchasing a new grand piano. Around this same time, the church had experienced incredible financial blessings. I had little convincing to do. Within weeks, we ordered a brand-new, five-foot-eight-inch, walnut-finish grand piano. After experiencing similar problems with our malfunctioning organ, we again wasted no time in shopping for a suitable replacement. Sometimes God raises the need for change by blessing your church. After a long season of having very few children in our church, God began to bring families with young children to us. As a result, we recognized the need to purchase suitable playground equipment for the children. Thankfully, we had plenty of money in the bank and everybody agreed that we had an obligation to accommodate the new families. When God opens a door and provides unity of mind within the church on an issue, lead them by making it happen; after all, people do change their minds. Don't muse endlessly over minutia when God has made it clear to everybody which direction to walk in. By refusing to act decisively, you may miss out on an opportunity to move your church forward.

Spirit-Led Change

Introducing change to your church, however, is not about picking an optimal rate of speed, be it slow or fast. If you are going to initiate change in a loving manner, you must walk in step with the Holy Spirit. Loving pastors wait on the Lord. I am constantly waiting for God to show me what the priorities for the church need to be. In any given week, there are a number of changes that I can involve myself in advancing. People come to me on a regular basis with projects that need pastoral leadership. Most of them are positive initiatives that could in some way benefit the ministry of our church. However, just because something is good does not mean that it needs to happen right now! Don't make the mistake of saying yes to every endeavor out of a sense of appeasement. Ask God to show you both what to do and when to do it. As we pray and seek the Lord through His Word, He is faithful to show us how to lovingly lead our church in accomplishing His will. It is truly remarkable how everything within pastoral ministry comes back to simply walking with Jesus Christ through His Word and prayer.

The Things You Can't Change

Although you may be able to effect many positive changes in your church, a powerful inertia to remain the same will likely persist. Certain things in local churches will not change in your lifetime. Don't let this upset you; instead, learn to love the people for who they are. Your job is not to achieve some ideal that you read about in a book but to lead your church beyond where they are. If you manage to do so lovingly, you have achieved much. Take your church as far as you can in the right direction, understanding that there will likely be many pastors after you to continue the work. Although God can do anything, He may not want to use you to do it. David's desire to build the temple did not mean that God wanted to use him to build it. Your successors will have unique abilities to effect change in areas where you are ill equipped. Pastor, keep the big picture in mind. Don't expend your precious leadership capital over things that do not absolutely have to change. If you alienate your strongest supporters over something that is not vital to the Kingdom of God, you will be greatly hindered in accomplishing the things that really matter. Never forget that your primary mission is the transformation of people's hearts. The various cosmetic features surrounding the institution of the church will forever be secondary to the all-important task of discipling people and sharing the gospel.

REFLECTION QUESTIONS

In what ways am I pursuing the kind of meaningful change that God desires?
Am I pursuing change in my church that does not matter?
Am I initiating change in a Spirit-led manner?

Chapter 6

LOVE YOUR CHURCH WITHIN CONFLICT

"A gentle answer turns away wrath, but a harsh word stirs up anger"
(Proverbs 15:1).

My sharp remark spread like wildfire in a long Texas drought. Within days, the entire church was buzzing over the incident. The conflict consumed every aspect of our church. Some sided with me, and others with the deacon's family. I stood my ground, believing with all my heart that I was in the right; however, I handled the situation like a fool. Instead of prayerfully and gently dealing with the issue, I rudely made my objections known. Some were angry and others were hurt. The church became spiritually ill and I considered resigning. What was the point of all the pain? After all, any job sounded better than being a pastor. I would have gladly traded the emotional turmoil for a job where you could clock in and out. The conflict created an intense mental toiling that followed me every minute of the day. My mind worked tirelessly to justify my words. My stomach turned sour every time my cell phone rang. Out of grit and determination, I resolved to stay.

During this time, I experienced tremendous academic pressure, in that I was taking a PhD seminar in Old Testament eschatology. My professor assigned three research projects totaling approximately forty-five pages of single spaced, in-depth research on complicated topics, which confused me even on my best day. The stress was staggering! One night, while attempting to make progress on my research papers, I found myself unable to concentrate on anything other than the conflict at church. I called my prayer partner and asked him to pray for God to give me an ability to focus. I will never forget what he did next. He drove out to my house and prayer walked my property while I typed my paper. He left only after I finished my writing for the night. Thank God for prayer partners.

The drama raged on, with neither side willing to raise the white flag. Something had to give. During this time, I continued to preach expositionally through the book of Numbers. One Sunday morning I preached about the Israelites grumbling against Moses and how God responded with lethal judgment. I preached boldly about God's disdain for grumbling, having felt its painful results. I presented a clear warning for those who dared to grumble against God's chosen leader. The sermon laid bare the sin of so many that Sunday morning. Still, nothing happened until I laid bare my own.

During the conclusion to my message, I told the church that sometimes it was easy to complain and grumble when you consider the profound imperfection of your leaders. I confessed to the congregation my failures in dealing with the situation at hand and, in a spirit of humility, I asked for their forgiveness if I had hurt them either directly or indirectly. During the time of invitation, the offended people came down the aisle to tell me that they forgave me. The woman leading the invitation song fell to her knees weeping at the altar. Another leader who had criticized me came forward to make things right. We sang verse after verse of the invitation hymn while God orchestrated healing in our fellowship. I must say, this is the closest I have ever been to genuine revival. Since this was orchestrated by God, the conflict faded almost immediately into the past. God restored relationships and brought genuine healing to our church.

Exert Both Strength and Humility

Pastors must be a formidable force at times. You must be unbending, uncompromising, and ferociously committed to God's Word. At times, you will face powerful opposition alone. However, the spirit with which you operate must not be pride, anger, or resentment. You must demonstrate humility as you hold to God's Word with all of your might. If your response to conflict is, "But I am right," there is a good chance you are in the wrong. Just because you did the right thing does not mean that you did it in the right spirit. Proverbs 29:23 teaches, "A man's pride brings him low, but a man of lowly spirit gains honor." However, humility does not mean giving up what you feel strongly about. Christ exercised profound humility even to the point of dying on a cross, yet He never compromised the truth. Do not miss out on the opportunity to see your own sin. God wants to sanctify you as well as your congregation. Be quick to humble yourself. "God opposes the proud but gives grace to the humble" (James 4:6). I hope you know how to apologize because you will not survive some of your mistakes if you don't. Please don't give the kind of apologies that direct blame elsewhere, such as, "I regret acting in such a manner that wrongfully gave you the impression that I was being unkind." Own your mistakes. Just say, "I am so very sorry" or "I really messed up, please forgive me."

One parishioner—who had assailed my leadership just days before—shook my hand on the way out of church and said, "What a great leader." Far from endangering my position as their pastor, confessing my sin endeared me to them. They had more confidence in my ability to lead them after I admitted my failure. One of the reasons we love David in the Bible is that he was a righteous man who made big mistakes. The honesty with which the Bible presents his life provides comfort to all of us who fail. Your congregants do not find comfort or encouragement by the image of a "perfect pastor." When you project that kind of persona, they quickly throw up their hands in frustration and say, "I'll never be as good as the preacher." If you project yourself as something other than what you are in Christ, you deceive yourself and others. Consider Proverbs 20:9: "Who can say, 'I have kept my heart pure; I am clean and without sin'?" Put more bluntly in 1 John 1:8, "If we claim to be without sin, we deceive ourselves and the truth is not in us."

Don't Add Fuel to the Fire

One of the worst things that you can do in the midst of conflict is infect your church with your toxic feelings on the issue. Proverbs 17:9 says, "He who covers over an offense promotes love, but whoever repeats the matter separates close friends." I know this is not a particularly deep thought, but please take it to heart: you do not have to say everything you think. A prudent pastor "keeps his knowledge to himself, but the heart of fools blurts out folly" (Proverbs 12:23) and a loving pastor "uses words with restraint" (Proverbs 17:28). Foolish pastors "delight in airing their own opinions" (Proverbs 18:2). Instead of talking incessantly about the issue to others, seek the Lord for understanding. Exercise extreme caution in all of your conversations, especially during seasons of conflict. Restrain yourself from sarcastic comments, rude glances, or caustic language that will only ignite the conflict further. Be especially disciplined in your preaching during times of conflict.

Don't use the pulpit to tell your side of the story, make people feel sorry for you, or rebuke those who have offended you. The last thing you need to do in the midst of conflict is to flog individuals with God's Word in front of the entire church, causing further harm to the church. Pastors who do this will raise the awareness of a problem that many in the congregation were blissfully ignorant of. Consistently dealing with conflict in this manner inadvertently allows a few parishioners to determine what is said from the behind the pulpit. Pastors who publically berate their church members from behind the pulpit forsake their obligation to deal personally with issues in a loving manner. If they do this regularly, they will create an environment where guests will never return. The more you talk about the problem, the more difficult it will be to lead your church forward.

Don't passively encourage the conflict either. Avoid the temptation to vent your frustrations on your favorite blog or social networking site. Don't tweet, text, or e-mail your woes to anybody even remotely connected to your congregation. Don't become the hub for everybody's vitriolic feelings on the matter by soliciting regular conversations on the issue in question. Make it very clear that you will not listen to people vent hurtful things about their brothers or sisters in Christ. Tell people you will be happy to pray with them or for them about the issue, but don't strengthen discord by encouraging gossip about your church members. You can console, love, guide, and shepherd your people without them telling you everything they know about a particular problem within the church. Train your church members to either remain silent or speak directly to the person who has offended them.

Small frustrations come and go in every church. Let them come, then let them go. Giving airtime to each of these will cripple your ministry. Avoid the urge to pull your staff aside to discuss conflict. Proverbs 26:20 says, "Without wood a fire goes out; without gossip a quarrel dies down." If there is nothing to feed the drama, it will likely die on its own. At all cost, keep the focus of the church on Jesus Christ and His heart to save lost people. When you think about it, church conflict is really symptomatic of a failure to focus on the Lord and His mission in the world. Maybe a difficult time in your church is a time to reinvigorate your outreach or evangelism program. The longer your church members focus on each other, the longer you will remain in conflict.

Not adding fuel to the fire also involves refraining from endless musing about the issue in your own mind. The more you dwell over inconsequential frustrations, the harder it will become to keep the focus of your ministry on Christ. You may be able to mull over the problem in your head harmlessly for a while, but eventually you will find yourself in a weak moment. It is amazing how something as benign as lack of sleep or low blood sugar can bring out the unlovely from within you. Not only will you eventually burst with whatever negative thoughts you are harboring, but you will most likely become bitter and cynical; neither sentiment is appropriate for a pastor. Hear the words of the apostle Paul: "Finally, brothers, whatever is true, whatever is noble, whatever is right, whatever is pure, whatever is lovely, whatever is admirable— if anything is excellent or praiseworthy—think about such things" (Philippians 4:8). Focus on the amazing things that God is doing in your ministry. Think about the people who are coming to Christ. Consider the transformational growth that you are seeing in your church members. Rejoice in what God is doing and avoid unnecessary rumination of the insignificant things that trouble you.

Remain Calm

Church conflict can be exasperating. As a leader, however, you do not have the luxury of voicing panic, despair, or annoyance. While in conflict, it is critical that you remain calm. Proverbs 17:27 teaches that, "A man of knowledge uses words with restraint, and a man of understanding is even-tempered." Your church members need to see their pastor trusting God. Do not shoulder the angst of those around you; show them something better. Demonstrate for them an unyielding trust in the Lord. If you waiver, you will cause your church to waiver. If you give up, they will too. If you become angry, they will become angry. If you gossip about church members in the midst of conflict, they will join in. If you are filled with fear, they will also give in to fear. If you leave the church, many of them will follow suit.

You must avoid becoming emotionally involved in the vortex of drama; otherwise, you will have a difficult time calming the tensions of those around you. I'm not encouraging you to be cold and dismissive about things that others care deeply about; however, it is critical that you react to conflict in a logical and objective manner. Encourage others to see the big picture. Those who are upset over something small have usually lost perspective. If you join their angst, you will only encourage the drama. Stay calm, Pastor.

Wait to Deal with the Situation

Try your best not to deal with problems out of emotion or adrenaline. Do not allow your natural angst to dictate how you manage difficult situations. I have found that I should never respond when I am angry. If the problem or situation is not urgent, it helps me to take time to cool off. During this cooling-off period, I frequently find that the bulk of my negative response to a situation was mostly emotional and not logical. If the problem still seems to be an issue worth tackling, then I try to handle it while in a calm, relaxed manner several days later. However, it is crucial not to let the cooling-off period become an escape from dealing with critical problems in the congregation. Your church trusts you to be the kind of shepherd that can wisely enter difficult situations with firmness, wisdom, and resolve. Hiding from uncomfortable circumstances will cause your sheep to lose confidence in your ability to administrate and ultimately cultivate a sense of cowardice in your own life.

Be a Peacemaker

When the conflict is between two groups of church members, your job is to be a peacemaker. Try very hard not to take sides. Taking sides unnecessarily may split the church. Your job is to be everybody's pastor during the conflict and after it is over. If you take sides unnecessarily, you will alienate church members and they will most likely leave. If the conflict is over a biblical matter, you will have to side with Scripture. However, most church conflict is not about scriptural matters. The majority of arguments revolve around personality conflicts, business deals, poor communication, and power struggles. Stay as neutral as you can in the midst of the conflict while you encourage people to recognize the legitimacy of opposing views.

After flaring tensions have subsided (only after), it may be helpful to encourage communication between the two parties. If the problem has not escalated to harmful levels, simply encourage them to talk through the issue. If, however, the situation has spiraled out of control, mediation may be in order. I strongly caution you, however, not to turn a localized problem between a few people into a church-wide discussion on Sunday night. Instead, assemble only the affected parties and facilitate a safe exchange on the issue. If you do not feel equipped to mediate, find somebody trained in conflict resolution to sit down with both sides at a neutral location. As a peacemaker, you cannot guarantee a smooth resolution to the conflict. Do the best you can under the circumstances, but understand that some problems become irreconcilable. Don't beat yourself up over something that you cannot do anything about. Jesus said, "Blessed are the peacemakers" (Matthew 5:9), but He knows that you cannot control the outcome of a situation. Love your church by being a peacemaker.

Confront Individuals

God's paradigm for dealing with problems within the church begins with confronting an individual one on one. Handling issues in this manner preserves the dignity of the person who is causing strife and keeps a relatively isolated problem from becoming a church-wide conflict that everybody feels the need to talk about. According to Titus 3:10, pastors should, "Warn a divisive person once, and then warn him a second time. After that, have nothing to do with him." Instead of complaining or venting about a person's divisive behavior, confront them in love. Failure to do so will eventually devastate the health of your church. Too often, pastors fail to confront divisive people because they think it won't work. Although not everyone will be teachable, I can assure you that confronting people in a direct but loving manner works. I can remember the shock I had after challenging one man with his contentious behavior after a Sunday morning service. I assumed that he would get mad and never return, but he showed up that evening for worship. He told me that he was not upset because I had spoken the truth to him. Never underestimate the power of truth!

Turn Away Wrath with Gentleness

While in the midst of a conflict, never respond in anger. Proverbs 15:1 teaches that, "A gentle answer turns away wrath, but a harsh word stirs up anger." Any immature, foolish, or weak-willed pastor can react with vitriol. It is a sign of strength, however, to respond with gentleness. Only "a fool gives full vent to his anger, but a wise man keeps himself under control" (Proverbs 29:11). A foolish pastor will give full measure to his ire. Take a day off from work, cry out to God, seek counsel from a close friend, but do not respond with anger. If you react harshly, you will stir up even more animosity in your church. It is amazing how a calm and loving spirit can encourage peace within the Body of Christ.

Use the Conflict for Good

God can use the problems in your church to accomplish His perfect purpose. The promise of Romans 8:28 applies to seasons of conflict within a church: "And we know that in all things God works for the good of those who love him, who have been called according to his purpose." How many times has God used an argument or heated discussion in your marriage to introduce more positive habits? Conflict can teach you a lot about yourself and the people you minister to. God may want to use the conflict in your church to sanctify you in ways you never imagined possible. Perhaps He will use it to bring lasting changes to a broken system of church government. Maybe God will use the strife to confront problems that have flourished in darkness for too long. God may want to spark revival in your church! Conflict always reminds me to spend more time in prayer. Sometimes we, as pastors, take the unity of a church for granted, and we cease being vigilant. Allow the difficulties to drive you to your knees in watchfulness (Colossians 4:2), being sure of this: God has something to teach everyone in your church during seasons of conflict.

Don't Run from Conflict

Conflict in your church is not a sign from God that you need to step down. Instead of leaving, consider allowing God to change you![10] Concerning the believers in the Church of Corinth, Paul said, "I have said before that you have such a place in our hearts that we would live or die with you" (2 Corinthians 7:2–7). Paul's level of commitment to God's people shames most evangelicals who prefer to only minister in situations when they are treated well. Rebel against the temptation to leave your ministry when things become difficult. As in a marriage, we commit our lives to one another with the words, "for better or worse, for richer or poorer, till death do us part." Work through it, cry through it, pray through it, but do not leave your church unless God calls you elsewhere. Continue to love, serve, preach, visit, and pray. May God grant you the grace to stand firm with great humility in the midst of conflict.

REFLECTION QUESTIONS

How do I need to respond differently the next time conflict arises in my church?
How can I use recent conflict to facilitate positive change?
How can I serve as a peacemaker in my church?

Chapter 7

LOVE YOUR CHURCH AMID STRESS

"But you, keep your head in all situations, endure hardship, do the work of an evangelist, discharge all the duties of your ministry" (2 Timothy 4:5).

purchased my first handgun as a pastor. Unfortunately, it was not for the love of recreational shooting but out of a desire to protect my family from an unstable individual who had acted in a threatening manner toward my son and me. On one particular morning, we hid in the closet with a loaded gun and hoped the unstable individual didn't charge through my front door. I would like to believe that this kind of experience is unusual; however, it would be naïve to think that other pastors have not felt the same way. I preached a revival for a pastor who at one time was held at gunpoint in his office for several hours. Within a few minutes' distance of my current church, several pastors have been either shot or beaten to death by assailants. Even for those who don't face such extreme experiences, ministry always entails a significant amount of stress.

The everyday stress of ministry in the local church is real! Heart attacks, bleeding ulcers, and other stress-related illnesses are not uncommon. I remember the ninety-three-year-old woman who disdained me with such fury that, even as her son lay on his deathbed, she refused to let me see him to say good-bye. After his death, I attended his funeral only to find her grievously troubled by my presence. To the best of my knowledge, she took this resentment to the grave with her. The worst part was waking up in the middle of the night and not being able to go back to sleep on account of the endless mental toiling. I would try to figure out what could be done to mend the situation, but many times I had to throw up my hands and say, "Lord, You deal with it." There were several occasions when I was so distressed over problems that I reached the point where I could no longer pray about it. It was not as if I gave up on God or prayer, but praying oftentimes prompted me to relive the situation. If I did, even while talking to the Lord, my temper flared.

Even when times are good in a local church, there is a pressure pastors carry around that few people recognize. Counseling, hospital visits, and funerals can be emotionally exhausting. I have been to so many funerals, too numerous to count. The pastor works to prepare people for death, and then he works to console the survivors. I will never forget the horror of witnessing a woman suffering from the devastating effects of stage IV lymphoma. Words cannot express how long and agonizing the process of death can be. These experiences leave an indelible impression and can begin to affect you negatively over time. I know this is not the case, but it feels as though each painful encounter takes a little piece of you. You can't help but see the faces of your family members when you look at those suffering. Sometimes you can't help but see yourself in their situations.

Divorce can also be a very painful situation to deal with. On one occasion, I remember pleading with a husband to remain faithful to his marriage vows. He refused and divorced his wife, falling quickly into the arms of another woman. Once again, the pastor is there before the divorce, during the divorce, and then he remains afterward to pick up the pieces. I saw people before they went to jail, while they were incarcerated, and after they were released. I can remember baptizing a man who seemed so earnest in his repentance. Later, I learned that he had used drugs intravenously that very night. Joy can quickly end in frustration. I now understand in some small way what Paul meant in his second letter to the Corinthians when he wrote about the pressure he faced. Consider the following challenges that Paul encountered in his ministry.

> I have worked much harder, been in prison more frequently, been flogged more severely, and been exposed to death again and again. Five times I received from the Jews the forty lashes minus one. Three times I was

beaten with rods, once I was stoned, three times I was shipwrecked, I spent a night and a day in the open sea, I have been constantly on the move. I have been in danger from rivers, in danger from bandits, in danger from my own countrymen, in danger from Gentiles; in danger in the city, in danger in the country, in danger at sea; and in danger from false brothers. I have labored and toiled and have often gone without sleep; I have known hunger and thirst and have often gone without food; I have been cold and naked (2 Corinthians 11:23–27).

After listing these trials in rapid succession, Paul writes, "Besides everything else, I face daily the pressure of my concern for all the churches" (2 Corinthians 11:28). I do not think that this final item on the list constitutes an appendix to the real suffering enumerated above it. I believe that Paul's list climaxes with the daily pressure that he carried around for all of the churches. The frustrating thing about this pressure is that you oftentimes bear it alone.

A TIME TO WEEP

The longer I pastor, the more I hurt with those whom God has placed under my care. There is nothing academic about ministering to people in their time of need. Last week I visited the hospital room of one of my sweet senior adults who is dying as a result of a tragic accident. I laid my hands on him and prayed for him and the family with tears and brokenness. This was not just an errand that I had to check off my to-do list. His wife of many years and his daughter were watching him slowly slip away. Days later, I met with a woman who was grieving over the sudden death of her husband. In pain, she shared with me what it was like to reach over and not feel her husband in bed with her. Her intense pain goes far beyond anything I have ever known. I can't fix it, but I can hurt with her and show the love of Christ to her family. Today, I struggled to hold back the tears as I preached her husband's

> *memorial service. I preached the glorious gospel, just as I did at her mother's funeral and her aunt's funeral. I have performed so many funerals and seen so much pain. I have watched death, and I have cried with those who face that suffocating pain every moment of their lives. You would think that at some point these funerals would become routine, an unpleasant reality of a job that I can do without becoming emotionally affected. But that day has not come, and I pray that it never does because God calls me to clothe myself with compassion (Colossians 3:12) and to "mourn with those who mourn" (Romans 12:15).*

In addition to the challenges you face in your church, you will also encounter personal tragedy, like any other person. Tim Morrow was the most loyal and loving friend a man could ever ask for. For years, we prayed together and ministered to one another. He supported me through difficult times in ministry and was always quick to rush to my aid when I needed him. Tim was passionate about the Bible and loved to tell others about Jesus. In the midst of another one of my busy workweeks, Tim accidentally mishandled his handgun and shot himself in the head. I have pastored people through crises for years but felt bewildered by being on the other end of a tragedy. I held his hand and sobbed as he lay on his hospital bed struggling to breathe. On that night, I couldn't be a pastor. Instead, I needed one. Thankfully, three ministers from Tim's church came to the hospital and ministered to me and the family till well after midnight. Tim died the next day, leaving his wife and three precious children behind. Who does the pastor turn to when he needs a pastor? Having lived the stress of the pastorate, I humbly offer you a few guiding principles to sustain you through difficult times.

Pursue Christ

Stressed-out pastors frequently neglect their devotional life with Christ. The sting of insults, opposition, disapproval, and gossip can drive pastors toward despair. In an attempt to cope with the stress of ministry, pastors turn to the things of this world, namely, television, hobbies, sleep, or even food. While none of these items is inherently evil, they prove idolatrous if you turn to them instead of to God. Sometimes my personal devotion to the Bible declined because I associated studying the Bible with my job. I wanted rest from my job. I did not want to think about the church, so my flesh fought against an in-depth personal time of devotion. Other times when God would reveal something to me from His Word during my quiet time, I wanted to hide it. I did not want to tell anyone about the precious thing that I had found. I wanted to revel in the newfound truth instead of instantly figuring out how to explain, illustrate, and apply it to other people's lives. Sometimes, I did not even want to talk about it with my wife. However, these personal feelings were only symptoms of my famished soul.

There was a time in my life when all I wanted to do was play the trumpet professionally. Although God did not ultimately call me to be a professional musician, for years I tried to become the best trumpet player in the world. I spent hours a day practicing rudiments, exercises, etudes, scales, and concertos in a small cubicle on the University of Oklahoma campus. Some days I played far beyond the point of fatigue. I maintained a detailed journal of my practice sessions so that I could track my progress and set daily challenges for speed, musicality, range, and technical facility. My commitment to the task of becoming a great trumpet player led me to travel to other cities—Cincinnati, Chicago, and Aspen—to learn from several of the most accomplished musicians in the world, hoping to glean some new insight into playing the trumpet. I sampled numerous mouthpieces in an attempt to find the ideal match for my embouchure. I rejoiced on the days when I could play the horn effortlessly and grieved on the days when nothing seemed to go right. I practiced through discomfort, headaches, stress, and fatigue. My disciplined approach to this egotistical goal in my life often puts my spiritual discipline to shame!

One of the most rewarding experiences in my walk with the Lord has been committing Psalm 119 to memory. I began memorizing the glorious Psalm in college and over the course of a year and half slowly memorized all 176 verses. To this day, I can still quote many of those verses without much effort. One of my favorite things about this Psalm is the author's passionate pursuit of the Lord through His Word. The psalmist seeks the Lord to the point of his eyes failing (v. 82). Has your desperation ever compelled you to search God's Word to the extent that your eyes began to fail? The psalmist pursues the Lord even when he is slandered (v. 23), mocked (v. 51), and persecuted (v. 161). Do you passionately seek the Lord even when it seems nothing is going well in your ministry?

Allow your stress to drive you relentlessly to Christ through His Word and prayer. Consider Paul and Silas who, after being flogged and imprisoned, sang praises to God in the middle of night. Pursue Christ, understanding that wandering for a pastor leads to the worst kind of hypocrisy.[11] You lose credibility with your congregation if you allow your personal devotion to deteriorate amidst unyielding stress. Commit yourself to a disciplined devotional life no matter what. Nothing else can give you the fortitude you need to prevail over the pressures of the pastorate. Don't join the masses of undisciplined pastors who sink into the mire of their circumstances. Demonstrate for your church members how to rise above the challenges and difficulties of life. You cannot minister with the power of the resurrected Lord while perpetuating a prideful, self-sufficiency.

Pour Out Your Heart to God

Over the course of your ministry, you will attend to people in tragic, depressing, explosive, violent, and unspeakable circumstances. As time passes, a pastor gathers a massive quantity of personal information about his sheep. This is exactly the way it should be too. There is no way to effectively minister to people if you do not really know them. It is a best-case scenario when a pastor loves his church to the point where they trust him enough to share even the shameful things they would tell no one else. Along with this information, however, comes a burden that pastors, in certain situations, must bear alone. As Solomon observed, ". . . the more knowledge the more grief" (Ecclesiastes 1:18). There are some things you cannot even tell your wife. Under these circumstances, you must learn to "cast your cares upon the Lord and he will sustain you" (Psalm 55:22). Take the grievous stories that people tell you to the Lord. Bring to Him the burdens that people bring to you. Talk to Him about the impossible situations your church members share with you. The stories of abuse, addiction, violence, and sexual sin will crush you over time if you do not give them over to the Lord. Pour your heart out to God, and trust Him to give you the strength to bears people's burdens.

Nurture a Support Network

You are not likely to survive the stress of ministry if you serve the Lord in complete isolation from a meaningful support network. It is in the best interests of your church for you to have someone to turn to for help and guidance. For years, I have enjoyed the fellowship of dear friends in the ministry. These are the kind of men I can trust implicitly to speak truth into my life and pray for me. We depend on each other for wise counsel and support in the midst of difficult circumstances. These relationships, however, don't just appear. You must nurture them through the years. Go out of your way to encourage your brothers in the ministry. Be there for them and they will be there for you. God will use your brothers in the ministry to encourage and sustain you through the difficult times in the ministry.

Give Thanks

Pastor, God desires for you to give thanks to Him in every circumstance (1 Thessalonians 5:18). Paul's admonition to give thanks in 1 Thessalonians 5:18 is not an anomaly in the Bible. Instead, it is consistent with a large chorus of verses that challenge you to fix your eyes on the Lord and not your personal problems. After being arrested, the apostles in Acts 5 rejoiced that "they had been counted worthy of suffering disgrace for the Name" (Acts 5:41). Pastor, "It has been granted to you on behalf of Christ, not only to believe in him, but to suffer" (Philippians 1:29). Give thanks, knowing that all hardship reminds us of God's love for His children (Hebrews 12:7–10). Give thanks that God will use the painful discipline to produce "a harvest of righteousness and peace" (Hebrews 12:11). God longs to mold and shape you into a vessel more fit for service in His kingdom. Consider all of the challenges of pastoral ministry joy, knowing that "the testing of your faith develops perseverance" (James 1:2–3). Thank God that He has counted you worthy of facing the difficulties of your job. Rejoice that God is teaching you the lessons that you must learn to be more effective in His service. Don't sink into the mire of your stress. Rejoice in the Lord!

Lead Christ-Focused Business Meetings

Business meetings can be so stressful. The open forum format used by many churches provides an occasion for people to express frustration over a wide range of matters. The structure of most business meetings also provides a stage for those holding minority views to amplify ill-tempered complaints. Overall, my experience has been that regularly scheduled business meetings can be a very positive and even beneficial practice for a congregation. One of the most damaging things to a church is unresolved problems that never receive proper attention. Holding regular meetings on business-related issues forces communication on topics that may be uncomfortable. Since most church conflict evolves out of a failure to communicate, ignoring an issue for months or even years can be detrimental to the health of your church. Problems don't just disappear when the church leadership chooses to ignore things. There are several things you can do to love your church through potentially stressful business meetings.

One of the best things you can do as the moderator is to keep the focus on the Lord. Read Scripture at the beginning of every meeting, then pray or ask others to voice prayers for God's divine wisdom and direction. After this, the church will have a much better capacity to operate in a way that honors God during the meeting. It will also help dissolve the all-too-secular attitude that some people have in matters related to church business and finances. Don't allow the focus of the meeting to be on money. Focus on the manner in which God has provided for your body and the congregational responsibility to steward those resources. Don't focus on problems and challenges. Focus on God's ability to do the impossible! Managing the Lord's resources in a wise, orderly, and effective manner ought to be a corporate act of worship.

As the moderator, uncertainty about the topics to be discussed can be unsettling. In preparation for the meeting, coordinate with other leadership to solidify the topics that need to be on the agenda. Naturally, that does not mean that people will not raise others. However, preparing an agenda does implicitly suggest that subjects worthy of corporate discussion be brought to the attention of the appropriate leaders prior to the meeting. When people do raise issues that are not on the agenda, lovingly listen to them. Always listen. Listening, however, does not mean that you need to enter into an extended discussion on the matter. Further, do not give the impression that the church needs to vote immediately on every subject raised during business meetings. There are procedural ways to defer in-depth discussion and action on a matter. In my experience, however, all you will need to do is explain that such an important issue will require careful study and prayerful consideration before determining the right step to take. A loving shepherd will not lead his church in a whimsical or capricious manner.

I think it is also important to occasionally lead the church in a more extended period of thanksgiving during business meetings. In other words, we should not simply treat prayer as a means of beginning and ending the meeting. God desires for your church to overflow with thankfulness (Colossians 2:7). Seize opportunities in business meetings to openly and unashamedly express gratitude to God. If He has provided in an abundant manner, remind people that every good and perfect gift comes from our heavenly Father above (James 1:17). If you do not lead your church in corporate thanksgiving, your congregation will likely take God's provision for granted. Ungratefulness is a dangerous posture for the people of God. Church conflict, after all, is a colossal failure of gratitude. Churches that enthusiastically give thanks to God on a consistent basis are less likely to act in divisive ways over things that just don't matter.

Over the years, I found that business meetings were a great opportunity to express gratitude toward people in the church as well.

Paul admonishes the church in Thessalonica to "encourage one another and build each other up" (1 Thessalonians 5:11). Show appreciation for those who worked hard to decorate the church for the recent banquet. Thank the deacon body for volunteering part of their Saturday to do their missions project. Recognize your Sunday school teachers publically for all of the hard work they put into their lessons each week. Every now and then, express appreciation for your staff members for serving the church faithfully. It is amazing how the tenor of a room can change when you are doing things God's way.

One of the most liberating realizations I have had about business meetings, however, is that I am not responsible for another person's behavior. God does not hold me morally accountable for what someone else may do or say, nor is it my job to make sure that everyone acts in a loving manner. I can only make sure that I act in a loving manner toward them. Beyond setting a loving example, my job is to moderate an orderly business meeting. Don't feel like a failure if coarse words erupt in the middle of a session. Continue to love your church and watch God change hearts over time.

Spend Mondays on Your Knees

Nobody prepared me for the temporary discouragement that often sets in on Monday mornings. The main problem is, of course, exhaustion. In my flesh, I usually want to sleep, eat, and watch TV after a long Sunday. Frankly, this is probably why so many pastors find themselves in such poor physical condition. I often feel as if I need to take a shower on the inside. There have been Sundays where my exhaustion has led to nausea. But it is simply not enough to say you're tired because the physical exhaustion pales in comparison to the emotional and spiritual drain that you feel. Sometimes, the better the Sunday is, the worse I feel the next morning.

One of the most difficult things about Monday mornings is the tendency to obsess over the previous day's interactions. I connect with so many people on Sundays about a wide range of issues. In rapid succession, I might speak with a grieving widow followed by an individual who can't wait to tell me a joke, followed by yet another person who is agitated about something. In the midst of these encounters, I might learn that somebody has died. Without faltering, I have to continue to be gracious to guests who have questions about our ministry. On Sunday afternoons, I am often in a situation where a committee is looking to me for leadership on an important financial or personnel issue. These are the kind of meetings where it is critical to communicate in a clear and cogent manner. Depending upon the subject matter, I may not be able to wait to return calls, e-mails, or text messages. Then there are dozens of brief interactions where it is important that I connect in a meaningful way with different kinds of people. God has put each one of them under my care, so if they feel it is important to tell me something, I think it's important to listen. Despite my best attempts to be available, however, some people grow weary of waiting in line and give up. Added to these exchanges, which all require communication, there is the preaching responsibility. If I have preached twice on a Sunday, I have used thousands of words. The gravity of that responsibility alone can lead to a considerable amount of exhausting introspection after the fact.

No matter how hard you try, not everything is going to come out just right. Everyone makes mistakes when they speak; however, most don't make them while standing in front of hundreds of people. The temptation on Monday is to worry about something you said or didn't say. Your mind toils over what they did or said and how you responded or didn't respond. You relive situations over and over to the point of fatigue. You say things like, "Why couldn't I remember his name?" or "I wonder if Bob took my comment the wrong way?" Do not spend your time worrying about everything that took place on Sunday. After all, the sin of obsessive worrying is no better than the myriad of sins you boldly preached against the day before. One of the most valuable things you can do on Monday mornings is to move forward. Mistakenly referring to the Midianites as the Gibeonites in your Sunday message will not destroy your church. You cannot change a single thing about what you did and said, or didn't do and say the day the before. Leave the past in the past and press forward! Fall on your face before God, and ask Him to give you the strength to move forward.

Face Criticism with Humility

Receiving harsh criticism about one of my sermons always feels like a kick in the stomach. Clearly, I put my heart into its preparation and articulation. After the exhausting challenge of delivering the message, you definitely do not want to hear someone say in a disgruntled tone that they think you were wrong. In my flesh, I always want to explain to them that I have given my life to the study of God's Word, spending years in intense theological training. I want to bring all logic and Scripture to bear as I explain to them quickly and effectually the folly of their criticism. I want to ask how they would feel if I treated the fruit of their arduous labor with such contempt. Yet all of these responses would amount to walking in a manner unworthy of the gospel (Philippians 1:27). As Baxter notes, "One needless contention, one covetous action, may cut the throat of many a sermon, and blast the fruit of all that you have been doing."[12] Again, your task in the face of harsh criticism is to keep a gentle, humble, and teachable demeanor. You do not have to concede the point you believe strongly in, but you do have to listen patiently to them. Your church members will never be teachable if you are not teachable. Be willing to consider that you are wrong. Think carefully about what they are saying, but above all listen patiently to them.

Moses demonstrated this kind of profound humility in the face of rebellious opposition. Repeatedly, Moses responded to the Israelites' complaints by going to God in prayer. The Israelites complained to him over not having the same foods as they enjoyed in Egypt, but Moses responded in prayer (Numbers 11). Miriam and Aaron complained against Moses because of his Cushite wife and, once again, Moses refused to answer them according to their folly (Numbers 12). In fact, the Bible says, "Now Moses was a very humble man, more humble than anyone else on the face of the earth" (Numbers 12:3).

Jesus Christ also demonstrated this profound humility in His earthly ministry after repeated assaults. The Pharisees challenged His right to forgive sins (Luke 5) and heal on the Sabbath (Luke 6), and they plotted against Him. Luke records that the Pharisees "were furious and began to discuss with one another what they might do to Jesus." The very next verse says that "Jesus went out to a mountainside to pray, and he spent the night praying to God." Although He certainly had the power to verbally decimate the Pharisees, Jesus refrained from answering them according to their folly. Jesus could have made them mute, or cripple, but instead, He prayed! In so doing, Jesus exemplified the Sermon on the Mount, in which He taught the disciples, saying, "Blessed are you when people insult you, persecute you and falsely say all kinds of evil against you because of me. Rejoice and be glad, because great is your reward in heaven . . . Love your enemies, do good to those who hate you, bless those who curse you, pray for those who mistreat you. If someone strikes you on one cheek, turn to him the other also. If someone takes your cloak, do not stop him from taking your tunic" (Matthew 5:11–12a, 6:27b–29).

You must lay down your "right" to be liked and live according to the words of Jesus, Who said, "Woe to you when all men speak well of you" (Luke 6:26). You will never regret holding your tongue and praying for a person who mistreats you, but you will always regret the harsh words that you spoke in anger or retaliation.

Wage Spiritual Warfare

A friend of mine served two combat tours in Iraq and Afghanistan as a Navy Seal. During his second tour in Afghanistan, he served as a Seal sniper. Exhausted from ministry and life, I poured out my frustrations to this friend in my office one day. God was blessing my ministry in an abundant fashion, but I felt like I was struggling in a spiritual slough. I told him I had no idea why I was having such a difficult time. With patience and kindness, my friend reminded me that I was engaged in spiritual warfare. Further, he made it clear that his sniper training had taught him to always aim his weapon at the "guy holding the radio." Coming from a warrior who was trained to kill by the most elite fighting force on the planet, his words pierced me to my core. Not only was I at war, but the enemy was aiming at me. As Baxter notes, "Take heed, therefore, brethren, for the enemy hath a special eye upon you. You shall have his most subtle insinuations, and incessant solicitations, and violent assaults."[13]

Scripture speaks of the devil as a roaring lion who seeks to devour (1 Peter 5:8). Zechariah paints a vivid picture of the enemy's assault on God's anointed. Called by God to rebuild the temple, Joshua faced the onslaught of Satan himself. Zechariah records in chapter 3, verse 1: "Then he showed me Joshua the high priest standing before the angel of the Lord, and Satan standing at his right side to accuse him." I am convinced that Satan verbally attacks pastors in a manner that causes inner doubt, conflict, and despair. Oddly, neither the angel of the Lord or Joshua responded to Satan. Instead, the Lord comes to Joshua's defense saying, "The Lord rebuke you, Satan! The Lord, who has chosen Jerusalem, rebuke you!" By invoking His own name, the Lord confronted Satan with the full breadth of his character revealed in the Old Testament. He might as well have said, "May the God Who spoke creation into being rebuke you. May the God Who rained down burning sulfur on Sodom and Gomorrah rebuke you! May the Lord Who redeemed Israel out of Egypt by miraculously devastating their entire empire rebuke you! May the God Who guided and sustained Israel in the desert for forty years rebuke you! May the God Who powerfully obliterated Jericho rebuke you! May the God Who repeatedly rescued Israel from their marauding neighbors rebuke you!" After invoking His own name, the Lord reminded Satan that He chose Jerusalem. In short, the Lord appears to be saying, "If you mess with Israel, you are messing with me." Suffice it to say that God has your back in the midst of spiritual attack.

It appears from the context of Zechariah 3 that Satan attacked Joshua not only because of the important task that God called him to (rebuilding the temple) but because he was not perfect. Zechariah 3:3–4 records, "Now Joshua was dressed in filthy clothes as he stood before the angel. The angel said to those who were standing before him, 'Take off his filthy clothes.' Then he said to Joshua, 'See, I have taken away your sin, and I will put fine garments on you.'" As the high priest, Joshua represented the most holy, righteous man in Israel. Yet, he stood before God as one wearing "filthy clothes." I hope you know that being a pastor in no way frees you from any struggle with sin. Perhaps your actions have given Satan plenty of material to attack you with. Nevertheless, God was faithful to take away Joshua's sin and clothe him in fine garments. In the midst of spiritual attack, confess any known sin in your life and embrace afresh the righteousness that God made available through Jesus Christ. Put on the breastplate of righteousness (Ephesians 6:14)!

Having witnessed Satan's attack, the angel of the Lord instructed Joshua, "This is what the Lord Almighty says: 'If you will walk in obedience to me and keep my requirements, then you will govern my house and have charge of my courts, and I will give you a place among these standing here'" (Zechariah 3:7). The high calling of governing the Lord's house carried with it the equally important task of obeying God's Word. So it is with you. Even while the enemy violently assaults you, your job as a pastor is to obey God's Word, being faithful in all that He commanded you to do! Walk with integrity before God as you continue to minister dutifully to His people. Stand firm in truth and be faithful with the gospel (Ephesians 6:14–15). Do not let Satan's attack discourage you from powerfully proclaiming God's Word (Ephesians 6:17). Do not allow the enemy to derail you from your responsibility to "pray in the Spirit on all occasions with all kinds of prayers and requests" (Ephesians 6:18).

Exercise Regularly

My accountability partner regularly asks me if I have been exercising. He understands how vital regular exercise is for my ability to handle the pressures of my job. It is not about staying thin. For me, exercising has everything to do with maintaining a healthy lifestyle that will enable me to function well amid stress. If I am not physically healthy, there is a good chance that I will give a sharp response under pressure when the situation really calls for a gentle, loving word. Nothing relieves stress like regular exercise. I have found a few creative ways to work walking into my busy schedule. I spend a lot of my walking time in personal prayer. For about three hours a week, I take long jaunts in a nearby park, during which I pray and rehearse my sermon. I conduct occasional meetings with staff members while walking. Why sit in my office, when I could easily have the same conversation outside while enjoying exercise? I even hold discipleship and accountability sessions while walking.

Find some sport or physical activity that you enjoy, and discipline yourself to do it as often as you can. The money you will spend on running shoes, a new bicycle, or a tennis racket will pale in comparison to the financial loss incurred by poor health. A gym membership will always and forever be cheaper than a trip to the emergency room or an MRI. Aside from the personal benefits that you will receive through exercise, you will be setting an important example for others in your church. Your members also deal with a tremendous amount of stress in their lives and, like you, they need to be reminded that they have a responsibility to take care of themselves. Loving your church means staying physically and mentally refreshed through regular exercise.

Learn to Laugh

In life, there is a time to weep and a time to laugh (Ecclesiastes 3:4); ministry is no different. You are unlikely to survive the ministry over the long haul if you only find the opportunities to weep. Other than being a great way to relieve stress, seeing the humor in a situation forces you to look at problems in a logical manner. After all, humor only exists when something deviates from the realm of normalcy. It's probably best if you refrain for the moment, but sooner or later you may need to give in to the urge. I simply had to laugh about the snakes that decided to attend the graveside service. As a pastor, nothing you say can be compelling enough to hold people's attention when a slithering reptile decides to make his presence known at such a solemn occasion. In this situation, ten out of ten times, people will ignore you and jump out of the snake's path. It's okay to snicker at the oscillating ceiling fan that decides to relinquish its decorative wicker pieces during a worship service. I couldn't help but laugh at one of my senior adults who loved to parade his dance moves during the worship service preludes just to agitate one of our ninety-year-old widows who believed dancing was a worldly pleasure.

You may also need to laugh at yourself. In an effort to relate to my church members, I have gone "coon huntin'" in the middle of the night and on a separate occasion was almost trampled to death by one of my deacon's cows. I've preached with a black eye, throw-up on my clothes, and poison ivy on my face. I've bungled a baptism and stood up in church with my zipper down. I have even had my car towed during an evangelism outing. In the climactic moment of one sermon, I mistakenly referred to the "Kingdom of *Heaven*" as the "Kingdom of *Kevin*." Although I kind of liked the sound of it, I quickly fixed the verbal gaffe, fearing the sudden strike of lightning. When you recognize the complete absurdity of a situation, you are more likely to face the challenges in an objective manner. Clearly, it is in the best interests of your church and your personal sanity if you retain the objectivity.

Take All of Your Vacation Time

You are absolutely crazy if you are not taking every day of your vacation every year! The relentless stress you carry around on a consistent basis demands that you have scheduled times in which you are totally unplugged from the ministry. No one can be on call every minute of every day of the entire year. Scheduling regular vacation times will ensure that you have at least some respite in the midst of an otherwise ceaseless flow of heavy responsibility. If you get into the habit of not taking vacation time, you will train your people to think that pastors don't need time off. A projection of this superhuman façade will ultimately crumble along with your health if you are not careful. If not for your own well-being, make sure you "clock out" regularly so that your church does not expect the next pastor to work without vacations. Not taking regular vacation time also communicates an overly developed sense of self-importance. No part of your ministry will collapse if you take a few weeks off each year. It is actually quite humbling to experience just how well things can "move right along" without you. If everything falls apart in your absence, it means that you have not done an effective job as a leader.

In my experience, routinely taking time off is a discipline. When you are accustomed to a demanding schedule, it becomes very challenging to make yourself slow down. I am convinced that God has allowed sickness in my life at certain points because He knew it was the only way to get me to stop. Sometimes on vacation it takes me a couple of days just to decompress before I can even enjoy myself. Rest is a discipline, just like work. Overworking yourself to the detriment of your church and family is just as sinful as laziness. Love your church enough by forcing yourself to stop and relax! You cannot stand to miss out on the blessings of rest.

There are a variety of blessings that present themselves as you discipline yourself to rest. First, it gives you the opportunity to gain more perspective on your ministry. If you never stop long enough to evaluate your ministry, you run the risk of squandering the precious time and energy that God has given you. You need time to ask reflective questions, like: "Why are we doing the things that we are doing at church?" "Are our efforts effective?" "What else do we need to be doing?" God may use your time of reflection to drastically change your course in ministry. The Lord may teach you a powerful lesson from Scripture that will dynamically impact every aspect of your ministry. We forfeit these teachable moments when we fail to take regular vacation time.

I have also learned that yielding the pulpit to capable men for a few Sundays per year gives your church an opportunity to miss you. I suppose it's human nature: we are all prone to take things for granted. If you faithfully love your church in all of the ways described in this book, your church will miss you while you are gone and appreciate you when you return. Perhaps you are fearful that your church will love the supply preacher more than they do you. This is a ridiculous concern. No matter how excellently preachers communicate the Bible in your absence, none of them can love your flock like you can!

I am writing this paragraph on behalf of your wife and children who desperately need you! A wise man once said, "Over the course of your career you will pastor several churches, but you will only have one family." Your family needs your undivided attention. The memories that you make while on vacation together will bless you, all your lives. To steal this precious time from those you love the most in order to feed some narcissistic, inflated sense of self-worth is despicable. Your children will resent you when they get old enough to realize that you were a great pastor to everybody but them. You cannot be a great pastor and a lousy father at the same time! If you are a pathetic husband and father, then you are failing as a pastor on the most fundamental level. Consider the example you are setting for husbands and fathers in your church if you neglect your family's needs.

Do Not Overextend Yourself

There is a sense in which the work of a pastor is never done. There is always another visit you could make or another commentary you could read, or another thank-you note you could write. As you walk with Christ, God will give you wisdom to know when it's time to put it all aside. I also encourage you to listen to those who know and love you the most. When my wife, church members, and fellow staff members begin to express concern about my need for rest, I know it's time to slow down. I remember talking with my wife on one occasion about my need to attend a ministry event. I suppose it was a busy time of year because she gently pushed back with a phrase I will never forget. After explaining to her how important I thought the ministry event was, she simply said, "Isn't it always important?" She was right. There will always be an "important" reason to extend myself beyond what is reasonable and healthy for my family. Your responsibility as a pastor is not to do every "important thing" but rather to faithfully execute the *most* important things.

I have realized that the effectiveness of a pastor lies not in how many things he does but rather in how many things he does not do. There is no shortage of horrible pastors who regularly work sixty-hour weeks. A pastor's job is to prioritize his activities in such a manner that he spends the bulk of his time doing the most important things. When the unprepared sermons, meetings, and lunch appointments begin to pile up, learn to prioritize. You do not have to get everything done all at once, but you do have to accomplish what is most critical. Do that most important thing first and attack every subsequent challenge in a systematic and measured approach. Without question, the greatest work you can do is preach the Word in a powerful manner on Sunday morning. When the administrative duties of my job begin to mount, I force myself to focus on the Sunday sermon. As you accomplish the most crucial task first, you will relax and be able to tackle the rest of your duties in a systematic and measured way. If on the other hand you manage to successfully juggle dozens of tertiary duties while leaving your sermon shallow and underdeveloped, you have used your time foolishly.

Consequently, this means saying no on a regular basis to many "important" things. For me, I have found Saturday evenings in particular to be a terrible time for me to attend functions. I desperately need a restful Saturday night where I can go to bed at a reasonable hour. Guarding those nights from social activity keeps me from participating in a lot of good things, but on the other hand it helps me to be ready and refreshed for the most important ministry hour of the week, Sunday morning at 11 a.m. Far from embittering people, disciplining yourself to complete the most critical tasks of a pastor causes your church to respect you more. Love your church by not overextending yourself.

Take One Day Off Every Week

I had been preaching through significant portions of the Pentateuch at my first church when my prayer partner confronted me with the fact that I was not taking regular time off each week. Somehow I had managed to admonish others about the importance of rest in the Old Testament but ignored it in my personal life. I had plenty of logical reasons for not taking time off each week, as I am sure you do as well. In our minds, we think that we can be more productive if we continue to work. However, nothing could be farther from the truth. Depriving ourselves of regular rest robs us of our most fruitful labor. Just because you work incessantly does not mean that you are working well. If you push yourself without repeated time off, you will gradually observe diminishing results from all of your hard work. After building the discipline of rest into my week, God enabled me to accomplish an incredible corpus of work. However, this is one lesson I consistently struggle with. There will always be a myriad of things that I feel a need to attend to either in the church or in the community. Guard your time off, not in a legalistic way but in a manner that preserves your need for regular rest and refreshment. Love your church by taking a day off each week.

Rebel against working obsessively in a manner that harms your personal health. Love your church enough to take care of yourself.

Excellence in ministry requires an ability to shepherd your flock even when you are under a tremendous amount of stress.

REFLECTION QUESTIONS

Am I managing fatigue in a sustainable and healthy manner?
Am I taking a sufficient amount of time off each week, month, and year?
Am I being a good pastor to my family?

CONCLUSION—LOVE YOUR CHURCH

"And now I will show you the most excellent way"
(1 Corinthians 12:31).

It was so hard to leave my first church because I loved them deeply. Having poured so much of myself into this sweet church I longed for them to have a great shepherd after I was gone. I didn't long for their new pastor to be a gifted rhetorician or a brilliant scholar. I did not pray for them to call an outrageously talented individual with awe-inspiring abilities. Nor did I desire a pastor who could lead the church to explosive growth. Having invested so much in the lives of the people, I wanted them to have a pastor who would love them and teach them the Bible. A pastor who loves his church will feed them God's Word. A pastor who loves will clothe himself with compassion, patience, kindness, gentleness, and forgiveness. A pastor who loves will follow God's leadership instead of pursuing a selfish agenda. A pastor who loves will pray fervently for his flock and visit them when they are in need. A pastor who loves will not run when things become difficult but will faithfully shepherd his church through trials.

Shepherding your church in a manner that glorifies God is not simply a matter of technique and strategy. Being a great pastor does not mean having a high social IQ or charismatic persona. Instead, it is a matter of love! If this seems like a naïve or pathetic strategy for a dynamic ministry, you have not truly grasped the radical biblical concept of love. Love is powerful. Motivated by love, God redeemed a lost world to Himself. Those troubled by the severity of God's wrath would do well to consider the ferocity of His love expressed throughout Scripture. As the great hymn expresses, God's love is "vast, unmeasured, boundless and free."[14] When pastors resolve in their hearts to love their sheep with the love that they have received from Christ, they position their church to experience incredible blessings.

The Most Excellent Way

Although people tend to identify Paul's instruction on love in 1 Corinthians 13 as a passage most fitting for weddings—and though, without question, the "love chapter" is applicable to marriage relationships—Paul's primary concern is for the well-being of the church in Corinth. Within the broader context of a discussion on spiritual gifts (1 Corinthians 12–14), Paul presents love as the most excellent way to minister to others within the Body of Christ, but this level of devotion will never take root in a congregation if the pastor is not setting the example. It's not about pastoring a church that knows how to get along. It is about shepherding and training them how to love. In order to teach your people how to love, you must demonstrate it for them. Let us now consider 1 Corinthians 13 as a mandate for pastors to love.

Wonderful Speech Fails without Love

Paul begins this chapter by emphasizing the profound futility of words when they are not accompanied by love. He writes, "If I speak in the tongues of men and of angels, but have not love, I am only a resounding gong or a clanging cymbal" (1 Corinthians 13:1). Paul's admonition bears considerable force when you consider the fact that pastors spend much of their time talking. Pastors teach, preach, counsel, reason, explain, encourage, and comfort. Without question, they must learn to communicate in a compelling and effective manner. However, the most rhetorically brilliant sermons will fail miserably if the pastor's words are not spoken with love toward his sheep. If your preaching is angelic but your heart is cold toward your people, your words become clamorous and offensive. Perhaps you have heard the saying, "It is one thing to love to preach and quite another to love those to whom you preach." Not only are your words useless without love, your gifts, your knowledge, and your faith are as well.

Gifts, Knowledge, and Faith Fail without Love

Paul writes, "If I have the gift of prophecy and can fathom all mysteries and all knowledge, and if I have a faith that can move mountains, but have not love, I am nothing. If I give all I possess to the poor and surrender my body to the flames, but have not love, I gain nothing." Writing within the context of explaining spiritual gifts in 1 Corinthians 12–14, we can be sure that Paul had an appreciation for the importance of spiritual gifts. God has uniquely gifted you to minister to His people. However, if you exercise your gifts without love, you have accomplished nothing. In the same manner, if you are more excited about showcasing the knowledge that you gleaned from Bible college or seminary than you are about loving your people, repent. Your skillful exegesis of difficult passages and ability to parse Greek words will utterly fail unless you couple that knowledge with a profound love for your sheep. I do not say this to minimize in any way the value of a theological education. Having spent over eleven years in seminary, I understand the importance of growing in our understanding of Scripture. Although I value the things I learned in seminary, I understand that if I fail to love my people, my knowledge counts for nothing.

Perhaps no one understood the importance of faith better than the apostle Paul who wrote extensively on the subject. That's why his statement about the uselessness of powerful faith is staggering: "And if I have a faith that can move mountains, but have not love, I am nothing" (1 Corinthians 13:2). God never intended for you to express faith apart from love, whether for Him or anyone else. If you are passionate about developing and casting vision for the future of your church but are not equally committed to loving them, you are *nothing* as a pastor.

In addition, your most sacrificial labor in ministry proves inconsequential without love. Paul writes, "If I give all I possess to the poor and surrender my body to the flames, but have not love, I gain nothing" (1 Corinthians 13:3). The countless hours, the long nights, the stress-filled days amount to nothing without an abiding love for your sheep. First Corinthians 13 seems to open in an extraordinarily negative manner until you consider the converse of the truth Paul is espousing: When you couple your abilities, your knowledge, and your faith with a robust love for your sheep, God moves in a powerful way! When you love, your words don't have to always be elegant. Sometimes, you don't have to say a thing. Love is that powerful. Great men of faith throughout Scripture exemplified both excellence in ministry and an enduring passion for God's people. Both Jesus and the apostle Paul were moved to tears by the depth of their devotion for the people God gave them to love (Acts 20:19; Luke 19:41–44). Love your people. Paul clarifies for us in concrete terms what it means to love in the following verses.

Love Is Patient

Consider your own spiritual journey to Christian maturity. How long did it take you to learn basic lessons about being a child of God? Did you read through the entire Bible upon hearing that first sermon regarding the importance of studying God's Word? If you are like most Christians, God exercised His patience toward you over the course of years, as you struggled to learn some basic lessons. The fact of the matter is God continues to exhibit great forbearance as He waits for you to respond to His instruction. That being said, do not expect your congregation to instantly embrace and obey things that took you years to understand and respond to. Instead, demonstrate patience with them by faithfully teaching God's Word. As Paul writes in 2 Timothy 4:2, "Correct, rebuke and encourage with great patience and careful instruction." Pastors pride themselves on their great *instruction* but rarely consider the importance of great *patience*. Loving your church means executing all of your duties with kind forbearance. I'm not impressed by the pastor who quickly accomplishes giant tasks in his church by being condescendingly forceful and unnecessarily confrontational. This mode of operation runs contrary to the way of Jesus Christ and is detrimental to the health of the church in the long run. It's not merely about achieving great things. It is about doing them in the right time and manner. I am impressed, however, with the pastor who patiently leads his church in accomplishing God's vision over the course of years and decades. I stand in awe of someone who never gives up despite the most significant challenges and setbacks. Patience is powerful and will always outperform fleeting fits of extraordinary strength. As the book of Proverbs states, "Better a patient man than a warrior, a man who controls his temper than one who takes a city" (Proverbs 16:32).

Wise pastors will extend patience to their church members. Proverbs 19:11 teaches, "A man's wisdom gives him patience; it is to his glory to overlook an offense." When we consider the concept of glory, patience is the farthest thing from our minds. And yet, the Bible teaches us that patience is a remarkable trait. Demonstrate patience with those who routinely criticize your performance. Patiently return phone calls and e-mails. Patiently make time to meet with those who need to talk with you. As an act of worship, extend patience toward those who have hurt you or a close family member. Patiently preach, patiently teach, and patiently wait for God to work in people's lives.

If you model patience for your church, you will teach them how to respond to you when you mess up. I have learned that those who talk for a living will occasionally say the wrong thing. After all, "Where words are many, sin is not absent" (Proverbs 10:19). Preachers talk when they counsel in their study, when they preach from the pulpit, and when they provide counsel over the phone. One Sunday morning upon learning that my microphone was not working, I asked a widow at the back of the building to fix the problem, saying something along the lines of, "She knows how to turn me on." Clearly, I meant that she knew how to turn the microphone on, but that's not what I said. On another occasion, following the death of one of our beloved elderly church members, I accidentally said something like, "Sometimes it's sad even when older people die." What I meant to say was that the death of a loved one can cause grief even when we know that their passing is imminent. It is so easy to say the wrong thing and accidentally yet mightily offend someone. Thankfully, my sweet church was patient with me.

Some of my worst speaking blunders came during our Sunday evening services when I was a little tired. On one Sunday night, we focused on the serious issue of abortion and unplanned pregnancies. Naturally, this topic relates to other social problems such as sex outside of the covenant of marriage. At the conclusion of the service, in my fatigue, I accidentally prayed for all the married people to remain abstinent. Oops. Then there was the Sunday evening when I mistakenly introduced the topic for the night as *e-vandal-ism* instead of *evangelism*. One of our more outspoken members was immediately moved to conviction and enthusiastically volunteered. Let me encourage you not to take yourself so seriously that you muse endlessly over every verbal misstep. Christ said to His disciples, "I will build my church and the gates of Hell will not prevail against it" (Matthew 16:18). Choose your words carefully, but know that if the gates of hell cannot prevail against the church of Jesus Christ, you are unlikely to accidentally destroy it by saying the wrong thing. Be patient with your sheep and pray that they will be patient with you. Remember, "Love covers over all wrongs" (Proverbs 10:10)!

When people are looking to you for leadership, there can be a real temptation to act impatiently. If you do not have a clear understanding of where you need to lead your church, do not act out of haste. It is unwise to launch your church spasmodically in any and every direction. You will waste precious leadership capital and time that could be better spent getting to know your church. There are plenty of things you can do as you await clarity on the unique direction that your church needs to go. During this time of prayer and searching, patiently love your church. Spend time with them; get to know them. Preach the Word of God faithfully, and He will begin to nudge everybody, not just you, into understanding where He wants His church to go.

Lovingly guide your sheep in the right direction no matter how long it takes. Impatience is a clear sign that you have a selfish motive. Don't ever put a time limit on how long you are willing to try. You were bought with a price. Consequently, your life and your time is not your own. Commit yourself to doing the right thing for your flock indefinitely. Whether it takes weeks, months, or years, lovingly point your church in the right direction. It is naïve to think that a few good sermons and heartfelt prayers will get everything on track and moving ahead. Remember, though, that patience does not mean that you lounge around the church office drinking skinny lattes while you wait for God to move mountains. On the contrary, it amounts to working vigorously in faith that God will bless your efforts in His perfect timing. Pray and wait patiently. Preach and wait patiently. Visit your church members and wait patiently. Forgive and wait patiently. Reach the lost and wait patiently. Plan and wait patiently. Confront problems and wait patiently. Counsel people and wait patiently. As pastors, we labor on God's time frame. You may be in a hurry, but God is not. Love your church through patience.

Love Is Kind and Never Rude

Have you ever been compared to a primate and proof of Darwin's theory of evolution? I have. Being in the ministry provides you with plenty of opportunities to show kindness. Always remember, you never have permission to be rude or unkind to a church member. Never. Ignoring a person by not shaking his or her hand or refusing to make eye contact is an impeachable offense. Never roll your eyes at them, mock them, or make fun of them in a hurtful manner. Never say anything disparaging about anyone. Never gossip in a derisive manner about any member of your flock. As Christ says, "If you love those who love you, what reward will you get? Are not even the tax collectors doing that? And if you greet only your brothers, what are you doing more than others? Do not even pagans do that?" (Matthew 5:46–47). God certainly expects more out of pastors than He does out of pagans. Those who have forsaken all for the gospel ministry must be unwaveringly kind to everyone.

Paul admonished Timothy when he said, "Do not rebuke an older man harshly, but exhort him as if he were your father. Treat younger men as brothers, older women as mothers, and younger women as sisters, with absolute purity" (1 Timothy 5:1–2). Paul could have used a number of paradigms to describe the kind of interaction that church members should have with one another, but he chose the family. More than any other example, the family exhibits the strongest and most loving relationships. If I was ever in a position to rebuke my father, I can only imagine the kind of respect and humility with which I would approach that conversation. Approach every conversation with older men in your church in this manner. Do not show disrespect to your deacon body whom God called to support you in the ministry. You will not soon recover from an adversarial relationship with those men. Speak to them as you would your father. Similarly, interact with the younger men as you would a younger brother. Although I never had a younger brother, I watched how my loving older brother treated me. He didn't speak to me with condescension or demean me in front of others. I can only imagine how this would have shattered my self-confidence if he had. Also, your interaction with older women in the church should model the relationship of a son with his mother. Having always been close with mine, this comparison bears considerable weight in my mind. Do not speak to older women in the church in a tone that you would never use with your own mother. Even if they have wounded you grievously, your job is to show kindness. Likewise, relate to younger women in your church as one would a sister, with absolute purity. The kind of protection and care you would naturally extend to your sister is the very same concern you should display to them. Paul's instruction in 1 Timothy 5:1–2 regarding proper conduct precludes rude confrontations with virtually every age group within your church.

If you are rude to your flock, you will see your sin ingrained in the lives of those you are called to love. Over time, you will begin to observe your short temper, sarcastic tone, and disrespectful manners mirrored in their lives of those you were called to help sanctify. On the other hand, if you sow seeds of kindness, you will teach them how to rightly respond to you when you say something hurtful. I strongly recommend that you never congratulate a woman on her pregnancy unless you know from a reliable source that she is definitely "with child." Giving credence to the hearsay was my first mistake. Acting on the flawed intelligence, however, was far worse. My exuberance quickly turned to dismay as she responded, "I know I'm fat, but I'm not pregnant." In my dismay, I somehow managed to sputter, "Wow, I feel very awkward now." Despite my verbal gaffe, she knew I loved her and she responded with kindness. Love your church with persistent kindness.

Love Is Not Jealous

Pastors are not immune to the temptation of jealousy. In responding to God's call to pastoral ministry, you have accepted a difficult path. Despite many years spent in higher education, it is highly unlikely that you will make a lot of money during your pastoral career. You will not receive a signing bonus upon accepting a new pastorate. Unlike the business world, your increased productivity will not always lead to a higher salary. Instead, depending upon the size of your staff, the addition of new members may require more work, more responsibilities, more evenings away from your family, and more ministerial duties on the weekends. You probably will never ever own a vacation home, and I sincerely doubt that you will go on many cruises, fancy fishing expeditions, or trips to Europe. Nevertheless, you will face all of the same financial challenges as those around you. Your children will require trips to the emergency room, glasses, braces, and money for swimming lessons. The uncertainty of some ministry situations will test your faith in God's ability to provide for your quickly approaching retirement years. Yet without question, the joys of the ministry far outweigh the trials and hardships that pastors face (Romans 8:18). Love never envies another for the things that God, in His perfect wisdom, has allowed them to enjoy. Confess the sin of envy, then repent and move on.

Closely related to the jealousy that a pastor could develop toward church members is the spirit of competition that sometimes arises between pastors of different congregations. At times, you may feel like you are working feverishly to no effect in utter obscurity. During these seasons in ministry, you will wonder why your sister church appears to flourish so effortlessly. If stories of another pastor's accomplishments unsettle you, you may have a problem with jealousy. Similarly, if you find yourself prattling incessantly about your achievements in the presence of other pastors, you too might be struggling with jealousy. Your comrades in the ministry desperately need your encouragement, just as you need theirs. A jealous and competitive spirit will drive a wedge between you and other pastors, isolating you from a critical support network. Pray for your brothers in the ministry. Support and encourage them, but don't compete with them. Those charged with the task of piercing the darkness of this world with the light of the gospel don't have time for petty rivalry. Love is never jealous.

Love Is Not Boastful or Proud

Few things in life are more odious to God or others than a prideful spirit. James 4:6 teaches that "God opposes the proud, but gives grace to the humble." The full breadth of God's power and sovereignty opposes pastors who are proud. According to Proverbs 16:5, "The Lord detests all the proud of heart. Be sure of this: They will not go unpunished." Love is never boastful or proud. Your church is not about you; it is about bringing glory to God by ministering to His people. Here are a few of the ways pride might try to creep into your ministry.

As a pastor, your job is not to act as though you have all of the answers. Indeed, one of the worst things you can do is to project that you have reached some higher echelon of spirituality seldom experienced by others. Aside from being totally deceptive, it is discouraging to your sheep to think that they could never be as good as you. I have learned to be more transparent in my preaching, discipleship, and pastoral care about my personal struggles. Such vulnerability endears me to my people because they contend with all of the same things. Let your church members regularly see you broken and humble before God, never prideful.

Pastors also exhibit pride when they refuse to accept instruction. God entrusts pastors with the sacred responsibility of leading His church. However, this does not mean that they are always right. Pastors sometimes have horrible ideas and occasionally make poor decisions. Sadly, pastors don't always respond well when they receive a helpful rebuke. Upon making mistakes, you can fittingly shepherd your church by humbly admitting your sin. Proverbs 15:31, reminds us, "He who listens to a life-giving rebuke will be at home among the wise." It is amazing how God can use even our failures to unify and strengthen the Body of Christ.

Even during the best of times, pastors must guard themselves from a boastful spirit. As a consequence of your visibility in your church and community, you will receive a host of praise that you don't always deserve. Use accomplishments to point people to the Lord. After leading Israel to rebuild the wall around Jerusalem in an astonishingly short amount of time, Nehemiah went to great efforts to give God all of the credit. Nehemiah summoned all of leaders, Levites, priests, musicians, and people to celebrate what God had done for them. Complete with sounds of cymbals, harps, lyres, and trumpets, the nation of Israel gave all of the glory to God. Nehemiah even went so far as to instruct two large choirs to march on top of the wall, giving thanks to the Lord. After marching around the wall, the procession stopped at the house of God, at which point, they sacrificed offerings to the Lord. When things go well in your ministry, be quick to give all of the praise and glory to God. It's also important to seize opportunities to recognize others who worked alongside you in accomplishing great things at your church. In so doing, you will cultivate an environment of thankfulness toward God and gratitude for your brothers and sisters in Christ. Your ministry is not about you.

Love Is Not Self-Seeking

Love is never about you; it is always about the other person. The implication for pastors is clear: your ministry is not about you or your career. Consider the words of James 3:14–16: "But if you harbor bitter envy and selfish ambition in your hearts, do not boast about it or deny the truth. Such 'wisdom' does not come down from heaven but is earthly, unspiritual, of the devil. For where you have envy and selfish ambition, there you find disorder and every evil practice."

Pastor, if you are only in it for yourself, you have embraced something that is distinctively evil. Further, your selfish ambition will lead to "disorder and every evil practice." I hope that the thought of leveraging your church for your personal advancement is odious and revolting to you. Regard every aspect of your ministry in terms of how you can selflessly love your sheep. Compassionately consider their needs during sermon preparation and while preaching. It's not about how great an orator you are but about how God can use you to minister to His people. Strive to preach God's Word in such a manner that people see the greatness of Jesus Christ alone. Don't parade your theological vocabulary or flaunt your rhetorical ability. Confess every desire to impress people. Selfishness is both obvious and abhorrent. Not only will your church members notice your narcissism immediately, but they will gradually develop an aversion to it. Worse, as I previously cautioned, they may begin to act like you. No, let your members see a man who will selflessly serve his sheep. "For even the Son of Man did not come to be served, but to serve, and to give his life as a ransom for many" (Mark 10:45). Let them see a man who does nothing "out of selfish ambition or vain conceit, but in humility" considers others as better than himself (Philippians 2:3). Let them see a man who "makes himself nothing" (Philippians 2:7). Let them see a pastor who consistently looks to the interests of others and who takes the very nature of a servant (Philippians 2:4, 7). Let them see a man who clothes himself with patience (Colossians 3:12).

Love Is Not Easily Angered

Let's face it; you are human. As a consequence of your humanity, you will get angry. Rest assured, anger is not inherently sinful. The Lord Jesus Himself became angry. It is, however, a sin to be *easily* angered (Proverbs 22:24; James 1:19) and to harbor that resentment (Ephesians 4:31; Colossians 3:8). It ought to take you a long time to get mad! If you find yourself in a situation where someone is angry with you, here are some practical suggestions. Most situations will dissipate once people have had an opportunity to calm down. So instead of responding in anger, why not say something along the lines of: "I can see you're very upset; let's both pray about this and talk in a couple of days." It is senseless to try to resolve a conflict when a person's emotions are running at a feverish pitch. Also, be in the habit of asking people to make appointments. Explain to them that you want to be able to give them your full attention and can't possibly do so in the foyer, right before you have to preach. However, some things simply cannot wait.

If the conversation is time sensitive and must take place, enlist a deacon or trusted church member to be present. Having another individual in the room will provide an extra level of accountability and protect you from false accusations. Then, instead of trying to press your point or prove you were right, be sure to listen. James 1:19 says, "Everyone should be quick to listen, slow to speak and slow to become angry." Put differently, "Do you see a man who speaks in haste? There is more hope for a fool than for him" (Proverbs 29:20). There is a good chance you will realize that you are not nearly as right as you thought you were. Listening will also give you a chance to catch your breath and discern the most loving way to proceed with the individual. If it's appropriate, thank people for caring enough to bring their concern to your attention. After all, apathy is far more insidious than caring deeply about something.

Finally, I would caution you to be gentle in these tense interactions. Just remember, "A gentle answer turns away wrath, but a harsh word stirs up anger" (Proverbs 15:1). Never compromise Scripture or the well-being of a congregation to appease one irate member. Stand firmly on God's Word as you deal with angry members, but never respond in anger.

Love Keeps No Record of Wrongs

Paige Patterson, president of Southwestern Baptist Theological Seminary, was kind enough to meet with me concerning a mission trip to Burma several years ago. After discussing missions, he gave me a piece of advice that I will never forget. In a spirit of gracious humility, Dr. Patterson cautioned me to never allow a "bitter root" to form in my heart. Having experienced difficulties in my pastoral ministry, his wisdom quickly resonated with me. Though simple, his admonition can be difficult to embody. Part of the problem is that pastors, like everyone else, face the temptation to keep careful records of the ways they've been wronged. It is one thing to observe patterns in people's lives for the purpose of protecting the future unity of the church and quite another to harbor unforgiveness. You will develop a volatile disposition if you do, making it virtually impossible to love like Christ loves. Your job is to model forgiveness and mercy.

It is a wonderful thing when God convicts a person of sin to the point where they ask their pastor for forgiveness. When this happens, embrace them, forgive them, and move on. Your sheep need to know that the matter has been completely settled. If you keep a record of their wrongs, you will become bitter and prone to use their past indiscretions as ammunition against them. You certainly don't want your congregation remembering your wrongs. Your unforgiveness could train them to keep careful records of your failures. Psalm 103:12 states, "As far as the east is from the west, so far has he removed our transgressions from us." God, Who is rich in mercy, does not keep a record of our wrongs when we confess our sin. Project this mercy to your church by not keeping a record of their wrongs.

Love Does Not Delight in Evil but Rejoices with the Truth

Out of a desire to avoid conflict, it can be very tempting to ignore ungodliness in people's lives. It is so easy to be silent when people live in habitual sin. Silence, however, leads to much greater problems. When the pastor neglects his role as an ambassador of truth, he leads his congregants in turning their heads as well. Over time, the sin becomes accepted, normalized, and ultimately embraced. The difficulty of confronting sin pales in comparison to the long-term, systemic problems that develop when we allow it to fester unfettered in our churches. A loving pastor will gently and prayerfully confront sin, knowing that love requires truth. I have found this responsibility to be incredibly difficult. Despite that, I cannot help but conclude that it is unloving to pretend that ongoing, habitual rebellion within the Body of Christ is acceptable. Love your church by speaking the truth in love (Ephesians 4:15). You will also have to show this same commitment to truth when it comes to addressing our society's embrace of sinful behavior.

If you love your community and your world, you will rejoice openly with the veracity of the Bible. Don't join the ranks of cowardly ministers who refuse to speak truthfully in love to a lost and dying world. There is absolutely no way for you to shine the light of the gospel in this darkness without a robust commitment to the truth of God's Word. If you love your community, you will not shrink back from openly speaking God's Word. If you love your world, you will rejoice in what the Bible says about sin and judgment. If you bow to the pressures of our world and remain silent on topics that the Bible speaks plainly about, you will make yourself irrelevant for the cause of Christ. Love your church by teaching them to take a stand for truth. They need you to oppose the increasingly aggressive agenda of the enemy. If you are afraid to declare what the Bible says about sin, you will instill a spirit of fear and timidity in the lives of your church members. The enemy is not ashamed of his lies, so why are some pastors ashamed of the truth? I ask you, who will speak the truth if pastors will not? Make no mistake; there is a cost to standing for truth in this increasingly secular society. But there is also a reward. I sense God's pleasure in me as I combat the lies of the enemy with His powerful Word. Love rejoices with the truth.

Love Always Protects

Love is never puny, feeble, or weak. It is a powerful and mighty force that compels us to shelter and defend those whom God places under our care. The love I have for my three children motivates me to protect them from all harm, and I would go to any lengths to do it. As a pastor, you will frequently be in the position of having to protect your sheep. The apostle Paul warned the elders of the church in Ephesus about the threat of wolves saying:

> Keep watch over yourselves and all the flock of which the Holy Spirit has made you overseers. Be shepherds of the church of God, which he bought with his own blood. I know that after I leave, savage wolves will come in among you and will not spare the flock. Even from your own number men will arise and distort the truth in order to draw away disciples after them. So be on your guard! Remember that for three years I never stopped warning each of you night and day with tears (Acts 20:28–31).

Day and night for three years he warned them to be on their guard. Do not take the unity or health of your church for granted. Contend for the unity of your church by modeling love, grace, mercy, and forgiveness. Paul knew that savage wolves from both inside and outside the church would threaten the unity of the church by distorting the truth. So how does a pastor protect his sheep from false teaching? The clear answer appears in the verses surrounding the above quotation from Acts 20. Paul said in verse 27, "For I have not hesitated to proclaim to you the whole will of God." After warning the elders about the wolves, Paul said, "Now I commit you to God and to the word of his grace, which can build you up and give you an inheritance among all those who are sanctified." Pastors protect their sheep by teaching and preaching the full counsel of God's grace. We confront the lies of culture and society by boldly proclaiming the eternally inerrant, inspired, and infallible Word of God. Through believing and obeying the truth of God's Word, our sheep become strong and resilient in the face of wolves.

Protect your church members. Never entertain gossip or derisive talk about any of them, especially your staff and family. Be loyal to your staff by always coming to their defense. Support them and they will support you. Protect your wife and children as well. They are, after all, part of your flock. Make sure they know that they are the most important church members to you. In fact, don't just say it; demonstrate it to them. Prove it by lovingly pastoring your family. Routinely put them first before other less important obligations and responsibilities. Protect your family, especially your children, from the painful things in ministry they are not equipped to bear. Their love for you will compel them to rush to your defense and scorn those who have hurt you. Don't teach your children to hate church by constantly spewing disdain for people at the dinner table. Show discretion in what you share with your family.

Protecting your sheep also means guarding the pulpit from anyone who might speak things that are contrary to God's Word. Carefully vet those you are inclined to invite to share your pulpit. In the digital age, there is no reason to be surprised by a horrible preacher. Find their sermons on YouTube or on their church's website and listen to them before you extend an invitation for them to come to your church. Another way to protect your church is to be exceptionally careful and prayerful about the ministers you hire. Since it can be extremely difficult to dismiss an employee, make sure you hire people with godly integrity. Again, the Internet can be useful in the hiring process. The world of blogging and social networking provides a wealth of data on many of your applicants.

Candidates who post questionable material on the Internet can easily be excluded from the interview process. Do your homework and trust your instincts. If it seems as though something is wrong with an applicant, there probably is. Protect your church from them.

You must also protect your church from unrepentant people who want to join your fellowship. Those who call themselves Christians but live in perpetual, open rebellion do not need to join. I strongly recommend implementing a New Members class in your church if you do not already have one. Three stanzas of "Just as I Am" is not a sufficient amount of time to consider a person for membership. If a non-Christian takes the class, you will have an ideal opportunity to explain the gospel. If a person is unwilling to commit even a few hours to a New Members class, it means they are not ready to accept the responsibilities that accompany church membership. Having spent years preaching against the severity of sin, it is unreasonable to treat open rebellion so casually as to accept unrepentant members into your congregation. If you joyfully welcome them into the ranks, you grant them the ability to make motions during church business meetings. How long do you think it would take for someone who demonstrates a disdain for God's truth to rally members to remove you as their pastor? This is not, however, about self-preservation. A loving pastor will do everything he can to protect his church members from those who claim the name of Christ but walk in darkness.

Love always protects the most vulnerable within your church. Don't allow your students to participate in events where common sense tells you there is likely to be a problem. Protect your young people by vetting every person who works with those eighteen years of age and below. Having heard firsthand accounts from pastors about the disastrous effects of sexual abuse within their churches, I plead with you to require background checks for all youth and children's workers. Protect the young people in your congregation by requiring two adults to supervise activities at all times.

Depending upon your church's size and location, you may also consider hiring security on Sunday mornings. Make no mistake; it is costly, but when compared to the devastating effects of a tragedy, the choice is easy. I have never regretted spending extra money to provide an additional layer of security for my church. There are situations that your seminary training just does not prepare you for. On one occasion, I sensed a distinct problem with a man new to our church. He seemed like a really nice guy when I met him, but over a short time his behavior became increasingly disturbing to me and others on staff. His e-mails, letters, and visits suggested that he was unstable. In certain situations, people with a deteriorating mental condition become fixated on the pastor; a trend that has nothing to do with me and everything to do with the office I hold. The peculiarity of his behavior and our inability to predict his behavior alarmed me. I felt so conflicted. On the one hand, the possibility of a violent act seemed unlikely. Yet, knowingly allowing an unstable man unfettered access to the rest of the church body seemed foolish. In this kind of situation, you need to surround yourself with people who can advise you. I am eternally optimistic about most situations in life, but my positive outlook is not informed by experience in law enforcement. In this situation, I resolved to listen to those who had the knowledge and training that I lacked and made the decision to be proactive. If your church cannot afford to hire security, develop a security team consisting of laypeople who know how to respond to security threats. Invite a law enforcement officer to come train your staff on how to respond to an emergency situation or to recognize when somebody is carrying a weapon. Strive to improve the security cameras in your facility. Each year, continue to add additional layers of protection for your congregation. Love and protection are inseparable concepts.

Love Always Trusts and Hopes

An insidious cynicism threatens to creep into the hearts and minds of vocational ministers who have experienced pain in ministry. Even passing conversations with some ministers reveal this disturbing tendency. Sarcastic jabs about one's congregation, though intended for humor, expose the adversarial posture of his heart. After a while, disappointment and discouragement can produce a sort of lethargy among pastors, in which they quietly resign themselves to accomplishing nothing. Such a defeatist mentality is not consistent with the pastor who is called to love.

Love always trusts and always hopes. Love never expects the worst of others but consistently looks for and expects the best. A loving pastor will not project his past frustrations with individuals onto how they may act in the future. Love always trusts that the truth of God is powerful to transform people from the inside out. Love always trusts that God is constantly at work in people's lives through the powerful ministry of the Holy Spirit. Love trusts that God will sanctify His people. Love hopes because we serve a God Whose infinite power is incomprehensible. Love hopes because hope is inseparable from faith, and "without faith it is impossible to please God" (Hebrews 11:6).

Love Always Perseveres

If your love for your church diminishes upon being treated poorly, you have embraced a worldly concept of love. The capricious, selfish, and emotional connotations commonly associated with love in no way compare with the enduring, persevering nature of the biblical concept. Your love for your church must never be fickle, circumstantial, or unpredictable. In fact, an abiding love for your congregants must be the most predictable thing about you. This is one of the greatest ways that you can show Jesus to your church. As Christ explained, hired hands will simply abandon the sheep when they see trouble coming. The hired hand runs away because he "cares nothing for the sheep" (John 10:13). In contrast, Jesus said, "I am the good shepherd; I know my sheep and my sheep know me—just as the Father knows me and I know the Father—and I lay down my life for the sheep" (John 10:14–15).

Instead of running at the first sign of trouble, love your sheep by continuing to shepherd them. Love them when they have criticized you or one of your family members unfairly. Love them after they have shown you disrespect or ignored your counsel. Love them even after they have left your church for selfish, unbiblical reasons. Love them when they ignore you. Love them when they call you names. Love them when they undermine your leadership. During the most difficult times in my church, I never once suggested to them that I might leave. Your church needs to see steady leadership in the midst of tumultuous circumstances.

Never threaten to leave, never talk about leaving, and never act like you want to leave. Demonstrate an unflinching commitment to love your flock. Let them know that your love is unconditional. Your people will flourish under your love, and you will cultivate an environment where people in the community long to be.

A persevering love is constant. Love, in its most fundamental expression, must be executed on a continual basis. Biblical love is not sporadic. The temptation is to care for your church in a lethargic manner, then attempt herculean expressions of love that you don't have the discipline to maintain for more than a few days. It is not enough to labor in prayer for your church members infrequently. They need you to cry out to God on their behalf without ceasing. In like manner, don't reward yourself for occasionally preaching a really powerful sermon. God's people need their pastor to diligently feed them God's Word.

I have learned that ministry is rarely about expending superhuman energy over short periods. Naturally, it sometimes requires such efforts, but the impact of your ministry is not the culmination of these experiences. It is virtually impossible to maintain this level of performance day in and day out over the course of one's pastoral career. Instead, the power of a pastor's ministry will be seen in his willingness to commit himself in a disciplined manner to much smaller tasks over long periods of time. Performing the right tasks diligently over the course of years can reap a staggering harvest. When it comes to test preparation, I have learned that it is not about how many hours I can cram information into my head the night before a test. Instead, it is about doing a little bit every day over a long period of time. Consistency will always outpace short-lived bursts of zeal and ferocity. It will also outperform talent, education, and experience.

Consistently lead your church in a loving manner. In whatever way God has taught you to love your church, do it faithfully with all your heart. Don't cheapen your call to ministry by always looking for some quick, superficial method to make you appear like a successful pastor. Take the path of love. Work the soil that God has given you and wait for Him to send the harvest (Proverbs 12:11). The path of consistently loving your flock is long and hard. There are no shortcuts to loving your church. Over time, however, the years of incessant sowing pay off, and God begins to bring the harvest.

MY PRAYER

Father, forgive for me for not always acting out of love for my church. Forgive me for every selfish motivation hidden behind my words, decisions, or actions. Forgive me for my impatience and lack of gentleness on days when pride overcame the responsibility to love my sheep. Forgive me for avoiding difficult confrontations that love for the Body of Christ demanded.

Father, thank You for Your amazing love for me. Help me to extend this love to every person You have placed under my pastoral care. May every sermon I preach be an expression of my love for the people Your Son died to redeem. May love compel me to do things for my flock that my flesh resists. May my love for them drive me relentlessly to my knees in constant prayer for them. Help my love for my church be constant, faithful, and unconditional.

God's Church Flourishes Underneath a Pastor's Holy Rebellion

As I have rebelled against unbiblical paradigms for ministry, I have seen people come to God through faith in Christ Jesus. I have watched people grow in their walk with the Lord. I have seen marriages mended, hard hearts softened, and relationships healed by the ministry of God's Word. I have witnessed the Spirit of God move in powerful ways. I have seen God grow our ministry numerically. I have seen God motivate His people to participate in ministry, both in our community and around the world. I have seen people take herculean steps of faith with me as I strive to lead them. I have seen God bless our church with an incredible measure of peace and unity. I have seen God give our members a strong desire to share Christ with the community. I have seen God renew a sense of joy and expectation in our fellowship. I have witnessed God create a hunger for prayer and Bible study. I have seen God create an atmosphere of trust where people share their burdens and encourage one another through their hardships. I have seen God invigorate Sunday school classes. God's love is so powerful!

It is a privilege to love God's Bride, the Church. If after reading this book the path of love seems trite or unimportant to you, I encourage you to find another profession. You can be successful in many other careers, but you will be an absolute failure in the ministry. There is no way for you to excel as a pastor without a genuine, committed love for your flock. Not only will you fail to flourish as pastor, you will harm your church. There is no amount of education, training, or ability that can overcome a deficiency in love. There is no excellence in Christian ministry without love for the people you serve. Ask God to teach you to love your church. If I struggle in one or more areas of ministry, I pray that I will never fail in this regard. Unleash the torrents of God's love by faithfully loving your church. Love your church with reckless abandon, and watch God do exceedingly abundantly beyond all that you could ever ask or imagine.

And now these three remain: faith, hope and love.
But the greatest of these is love.
(1 Corinthians 13:13)

REFLECTION QUESTIONS

In what ways does my love fall short of the demands of 1 Corinthians 13?
What are some specific steps that I need to take to become a more loving pastor?
How can I teach these lessons about love to another minister?

ENDNOTES

1   Walter C. Kaiser, "The Crisis in Expository Preaching Today," *Preaching* 11 (1995): 6.

2   Albert Mohler, "In Season and out of Season: The Centrality of Scripture in Preaching," *Faith and Mission*," 14 (1997): 79.

3   Oswald Chambers, *My Utmost for His Highest* (Uhrichsville, OH: Barbour and Company, 1992), 144–45.

4   Kaiser, "The Crises in Expository Preaching Today," 4–12.

5   John Piper, *Brothers We Are Not Professionals* (Nashville: Broadman and Holman, 2002), 2.

6   Paul W. Powell, *Shepherding the Sheep in Smaller Churches* (Dallas: Annuity Board, 1995), 39.

7   Stephen Olford, *Anointed Expository Preaching* (Nashville: Broadman and Holman Publishers, 1998), 47. Olford cites a lack of discipline not only in personal devotion but with family prayers, with food, in exercise, in listening to others, and in spending time with family.

8   Richard Baxter, *The Reformed Pastor* (Great Britain: BPCC Hazell Books, 1989), 76–7.

9   Ibid.

10   James W. Bryant and Mac Brunson, *The New Guidebook for Pastors* (Nashville: Broadman and Holman, 2007), 208.

11   Baxter, *The Reformed Pastor*, 76–7.

12   Ibid., 63.

13   Ibid., 74.

14   Words by Samuel Trevor Francis, music by Thoro Harris, "Oh, the Deep, Deep Love of Jesus," Music ©1931. Renewed by Mrs. Thoro Harris. Nazarene Publishing House, owner.

Other Pastoral Resources by Innovo Publishing

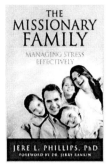

THE MISSIONARY FAMILY: MANAGING STRESS EFFECTIVELY by Dr. Jere Phillips, PhD. 978-1-61314-180-9, $14.95 Paperback.

Hundreds of missionaries go home each year due to stress affecting themselves and/or their families. Hundreds of others remain on the field but struggle with reduced effectiveness from bearing the burden of stress. *The Missionary Family: Managing Stress Effectively* provides sound biblical and practical principles to help missionaries and their family members manage stress and become more effective in ministry.

PASTORAL MINISTRIES FOR THE NEXT GENERATION by Dr. Jere Phillips, PhD. 978-1-61314-995-9, $14.95 Paperback.

How does a new generation of pastors and church planters make the most of unprecedented opportunities and build on solid biblical foundations of previous generations, while at the same time avoiding the pitfalls of perilous problems previous generations did not encounter? *Pastoral Ministries for the Next Generation* offers ideas from the best practices of the past along with promising concepts for the future.

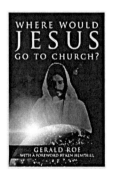

WHERE WOULD JESUS GO TO CHURCH by Gerald Roe. 978-1-61314-065-9, $15.95 Paperback.

For the blessings of God to rest upon any congregation, the church must answer two important questions: What is the true church? and What is the church to do? In far too many instances, these questions are being asked in the reverse order, leading to a compromising disconnect between the church's essential biblical character and its earthly effectiveness. *Where Would Jesus Go to Church?* sheds needed light and offers practical, biblical answers.

ABOUT INNOVO PUBLISHING LLC

Innovo Publishing LLC is a full-service Christian publishing company serving the Christian and wholesome markets. Innovo creates, distributes, and markets quality books, eBooks, audiobooks, music, and film through traditional and innovative publishing models and services. Innovo provides distribution, marketing, and automated order fulfillment through a network of thousands of physical and online wholesalers, retailers, bookstores, music stores, schools, and libraries worldwide. Innovo provides a unique combination of traditional publishing, co-publishing, and independent (self) publishing arrangements that allow authors, artists, and organizations to accomplish their personal, organizational, and philanthropic publishing goals. Visit Innovo Publishing's web site at www.innovopublishing.com or email Innovo at info@innovopublishing.com.

CPSIA information can be obtained
at www.ICGtesting.com
Printed in the USA
FFOW05n1929291014